Multilateral Development Finance 2026

OECD
BETTER POLICIES FOR BETTER LIVES

This work is published under the responsibility of the Secretary-General of the OECD. The opinions expressed and arguments employed herein do not necessarily reflect the official views of the Member countries of the OECD.

This document, as well as any data and map included herein, are without prejudice to the status of or sovereignty over any territory, to the delimitation of international frontiers and boundaries and to the name of any territory, city or area.

Please cite this publication as:
OECD (2026), *Multilateral Development Finance 2026*, OECD Publishing, Paris, https://doi.org/10.1787/0720370a-en.

ISBN 978-92-64-79690-4 (print)
ISBN 978-92-64-48944-8 (PDF)
ISBN 978-92-64-42348-0 (HTML)

Multilateral Development Finance
ISSN 3008-1890 (online)

Photo credits: Cover © plej92/Getty Images.

Corrigenda to OECD publications may be found at: https://www.oecd.org/en/publications/support/corrigenda.html.

Foreword

This report, *Multilateral Development Finance 2026*, is the fifth in a series that examines how the multilateral development system is resourced and delivers development support. Previously published under the title *Multilateral Aid*, this series provides a comprehensive view of multilateral development finance and its evolving role, scale and structure within the broader development co-operation architecture.

The report offers a unique systemic perspective by examining both inflows to multilateral development organisations and the outflows these organisations channel towards development activities. It covers the different components of the multilateral development system, including the United Nations Development System (UNDS), multilateral development banks, vertical funds, and other multilateral institutions, including the European Union institutions and the International Monetary Fund.

The analysis draws primarily on data reported to the OECD Creditor Reporting System (CRS), complemented by information on funding to the UNDS provided by the United Nations Department of Economic and Social Affairs, various survey results, as well as publicly available data from individual multilateral institutions.

The report is structured in four chapters. Chapter 1 provides an overview of the main findings, including a summary of the recommendations. Chapter 2 discusses the context in which multilateral development finance operates. Chapter 3 explores recent trends in the funding *to* multilateral development organisations (inflows). Chapter 4 explores the development activities financed *by* the system (outflows).

Acknowledgements

This report was prepared under the responsibility of Pilar Garrido, Director for Development Co-operation, OECD, by a team in the Development Co-operation Directorate (DCD) comprised of Leonardo Altieri, Clémence Decisy, Abdoulaye Fabregas and Marius Guérin under the overall supervision of Henri-Bernard Solignac-Lecomte (Head of Unit, Architecture and Analysis) and Olivier Cattaneo (Special Advisor to the Director). Jieun Kim provided advice on policy analysis at various stages of the drafting process. Harsh Desai and Ogulcan Ertunc provided guidance on statistical approaches.

The report has benefitted from the contributions of many colleagues. Emily Bosch, Olivier Bouret, Eleanor Carey, Tea Cimini, Harsh Desai, Ogulcan Ertunc, Cyprien Fabre, Anthony Kiernan, Jieun Kim, Rachel Morris, Valentina Orru, Cecilia Piemonte and Lou Turroques (DCD), and Laura Castillo Gutiérrez, Gaia Castori, Cecilia Corsini, Erik Engberg, Edward Hainsworth, Erika MacLaughlin, William Norris, Patrick Saez and Carolina Testoni (MOPAN) have all significantly helped improve the report and the authors are grateful for their substantive comments.

The report benefitted from consultations with external partners from research institutes, academia and multilateral organisations, including: Dag Hammarskjöld Foundation, University of Glasgow, United Nations Development Coordination Office, UNESCO and the German Development Evaluation Institute (DEval). Members of the OECD Development Assistance Committee (DAC) provided overall strategic guidance.

Katie Black, Meria Greco, Angie Lee and Rai Santana facilitated the publication and communications process, and Joelle Bassoul provided strategic communications advice. The authors are also grateful for the support received from Stephanie Coic on graphic design and from Aline Renert-Djian on administrative co-ordination, as well as for the editorial support provided by Fiona Hinchcliffe.

Table of contents

FIGURES

TABLES

BOXES

Abbreviations and acronyms

ADF	African Development Fund
AfDB	African Development Bank
AsDB	Asian Development Bank
AsDF	Asian Development Fund
AIIB	Asian Infrastructure Investment Bank
CAF	Corporación Andina de Fomento
CIF	Climate Investment Fund
CERF	Central Emergency Response Fund
CRS	Creditor Reporting System
DAC	Development Assistance Committee
EIB	European Investment Bank
EU	European Union
FAO	United Nations Food and Agriculture Organization
FCAS	Fragility and conflict-affected settings
FfD	International Conference on Financing for Development
FSO	Fund for Special Operations
GAVI	Global Alliance for Vaccines and Immunization
GCF	Green Climate Fund
GEF	Global Environment Facility
GGGI	Global Green Growth Institute
GNI	Gross National Income
GPEDC	Global Partnership for Effective Development Co-operation
IaDB	Inter American Development Bank
IBRD	International Bank for Reconstruction and Development
IDA	International Development Association
IFAD	International Fund for Agricultural Development
IFC	International Finance Corporation
IFIs	International financial institutions
IFFIm	International Finance Facility for Immunisation Company
ILO	International Labour Organization
IMF	International Monetary Fund
IOM	International Organization for Migration
ITC	International Trade Centre
ITU	International Telecommunication Union
L&D	Learning and Development
LDC	Least developed country
LIC	Low-income country
LMIC	Lower-middle income country
MDB	Multilateral development bank
MDO	Multilateral development organisation
MIGA	Multilateral Investment Guarantee Agency
MOPAN	Multilateral Organisation Performance Assessment Network

NDF	Nordic Development Fund
OCHA	United Nations Office for the Coordination of Humanitarian Affairs
OECD	Organisation for Economic Co-operation and Development
ODA	Official development assistance
ODF	Official development finance
OOF	Other official flows
PAHO	Pan American Health Organization
PBF	Peacebuilding Fund
RDB	Regional development bank
RST	Resilience and Sustainability Trust
SPA	Sevilla Platform for Action
t-SNE	t-Distributed Stochastic Neighbour Embedding
UK	United Kingdom
UMIC	Upper-middle income country
UNAIDS	Joint United Nations Programme on HIV and AIDS
UNDESA	United Nations Department of Economic and Social Affairs
UNDP	United Nations Development Programme
UNDRR	UN Office for Disaster Risk Reduction
UNDS	United Nations Development System
UNEP	United Nations Environment Programme
UNESCO	United Nations Educational, Scientific and Cultural Organization
UNFPA	United Nations Population Fund
UNHCR	United Nations High Commissioner for Refugees
UNICEF	United Nations Children's Fund
UNIDO	United Nations Industrial Development Organization
UNODC	United Nations Office on Drugs and Crime
UNRWA	United Nations Relief and Works Agency for Palestine Refugees in the Near East
UNV	United Nations Volunteers
US	United States of America
USD	United States dollar
WBG	World Bank Group
WFP	World Food Programme
WHO	World Health Organization
WIPO	World Intellectual Property Organization

Executive summary

For decades, the multilateral development system has expanded in scope, financing capacity and institutional complexity, but that trend is reversing. Since its post-war origins in 1945, new organisations and funds have been layered onto the original architecture to address emerging challenges, creating over time a diverse but intricate system. Originally designed to support post-war reconstruction and long-term development, the system has since been used to address an expanding range of global challenges. While this expansion was sustained by strong political support for multilateralism and growing development budgets, these conditions no longer hold. The system is entering a period of retrenchment that is exposing long-standing structural challenges and forcing a reassessment of its architecture, funding and role.

A turning point for multilateral development finance

The multilateral development system has reached a turning point. After decades of expansion, growth in multilateral contributions has reversed and long-standing structural challenges are becoming more visible. In 2024, contributions to multilateral development organisations by the members of the Development Assistance Committee (DAC) fell by more than 15%. Overall, projections suggest that multilateral contributions could decline by 23-30% by 2027, signalling a sustained reversal rather than a temporary correction.

This reversal exposes some of the system's long-standing structural vulnerabilities, including its heavy reliance on a small group of major donors. In 2025, 11 DAC members, accounting for roughly two-thirds of total DAC contributions to the multilateral development system, announced aid cuts. These simultaneous cuts by several of the largest contributors underline how the correlated decisions of major donors can compound to form a severe system-wide shock.

In this environment, donor choices involve difficult trade-offs between financing volume and concessionality, with potential system-wide effects. A smaller funding envelope cannot preserve both the system's overall financing volumes and its highly concessional resources. How cuts are allocated therefore matters as much as their scale: prioritising contributions that can be leveraged may preserve total volume but can shift the balance away from concessional finance. Protecting concessionality safeguards poorer contexts but implies lower aggregate outflows.

Outflows resilience masks growing pressure beneath the surface

The latest figures available at the time of writing this report (March 2026) show that multilateral outflows have remained strong, but this reflects delayed adjustment rather than underlying stability. Total multilateral outflows reached a record USD 296 billion in 2024, supported by the expanded lending capacity of multilateral development banks (MDBs) and the buffering effects of replenishment cycles and balance sheet financing models. While these mechanisms can preserve the system's delivery capacity in the short term, they merely delay the full impact of deteriorating inflows.

Signs of strain are already showing in parts of the system. Although lending volumes have continued to expand among some MDBs, several grant-based UN entities have already experienced stagnation or decline in outflows since 2022, with particularly pronounced contractions among large humanitarian agencies. Across the system, organisations report programme delays, reduced geographic coverage and lower delivery targets as they absorb funding shocks through hiring freezes, expenditure deferrals and cost containment measures.

The risks are magnified by the system's interdependence, raising the prospect of a collapse in multilateral delivery capacity. Multilateral development organisations operate as an interconnected network, relying on each other's resources, implementing capacity and normative functions. When funding disruptions affect highly central institutions, impacts propagate across the system and can disrupt the multilateral delivery chain. Moreover, the leverage power of some organisations, a major strength of the system in normal times, can also amplify vulnerability: defunding leveraged mechanisms, such as MDB concessional windows, can generate reverse leverage effects, whereby relatively small reductions in donor contributions translate into disproportionately larger declines in financing for developing countries.

Stronger together: An agenda to reset the multilateral development system

The system's future will depend less on the scale of contraction than on the quality of the collective response of its member states and multilateral organisations. A period of fiscal constraint can either accelerate fragmentation or catalyse a more disciplined, strategically aligned and resilient multilateral architecture. While efficiency reforms can help stabilise institutions financially, multilateral effectiveness depends on restoring trust and aligning incentives for collective action. Today, incentives are moving in the opposite direction: as donors seek greater control and organisations compete for limited resources, behaviours increasingly resemble a prisoner's dilemma, where individually rational choices generate collectively weaker outcomes. Member states and multilateral development organisations share the responsibility for safeguarding the system's collective outcomes.

The following recommendations can help to achieve this:

Preserving the system's delivery capacity will require co-ordinated action by member states to protect its financial foundations and manage funding cuts intentionally. This requires protecting flexible and predictable funding, which is indispensable to the system's integrity and effectiveness. Voluntary contributions should reinforce, rather than fragment or displace, core mandates. Member states should also rebalance burden-sharing to reduce excessive reliance on a small number of donors and manage funding reductions strategically, with attention to systemic spillovers. Greater transparency and forward visibility on planned funding changes would further help mitigate potentially destabilising effects of funding cuts and support more orderly adjustment across the system.

Enhancing the system's effectiveness will require multilateral organisations to pursue reforms that sharpen rather than dilute their development additionality and strengthen system-wide coherence. This includes reinforcing mandate discipline, clarifying comparative advantages and rationalising institutional arrangements to reduce fragmentation and restore complementarity and coherence after decades of incremental expansion. Where financing alternatives remain limited, concessional resources should be prioritised for low-income and vulnerable contexts. Organisations should also assess and communicate the operational and distributional implications of funding cuts. Making allocation trade-offs more explicit would strengthen accountability and help preserve development impact under tighter resource constraints.

1 Overview

This 2026 edition of the *Multilateral Development Finance* report examines a system at a pivotal moment of its existence. After decades of expansion, the multilateral development system is facing a convergence of pressures, including declining trust in multilateralism, tightening aid budgets and growing scrutiny of value for money. Drawing on OECD data and forward-looking projections, this overview chapter assesses recent trends in multilateral inflows and outflows, highlighting that despite record delivery volumes, funding cuts – if indiscriminate and uncoordinated – could have disproportionate consequences, especially for low-income and vulnerable countries. It makes recommendations for how the current moment can be used as an opportunity to reset multilateral development finance around clearer principles and co-ordinated action.

1.1. The multilateral development system, built for scale and complementarity, is facing multiple pressures

1.1.1. Development co-operation covers a wide spectrum of needs, risks and financing contexts

The multilateral development system has expanded steadily since its inception in the aftermath of the Second World War. Over decades, countries have established new multilateral institutions to address emerging development challenges, adding successive layers of mandates and institutional complexity. This gradual process has produced a diverse yet intricate architecture. In the past two decades alone, the number of multilateral development organisations (MDOs) has nearly doubled, reaching more than 200 entities by 2020 (OECD, 2024[1]).

Today, the multilateral development system is a core pillar of the development co-operation architecture. MDOs have been receiving and channelling a growing share of development co-operation from the members of the OECD Development Assistance Committee (DAC): in 2024, 41% of DAC members' official development assistance (ODA) was delivered to or through the multilateral development system, up from 37% in 2010. Bilateral donors have thus been increasingly relying on multilateral mechanisms to support the global development agenda.

Beyond this growing importance as a channel of ODA, the system also delivers value that no individual donor could achieve alone: global reach (including in high fragility and conflict-affected contexts), the ability to deliver at scale (through resource pooling and capital leveraging), and specialised expertise (in areas ranging from humanitarian response to infrastructure finance and global public goods).

The system's unique value allows it to operate across a broad range of needs, risks and financing contexts. Collectively, MDOs support countries at every development stage, from delivering essential services and humanitarian assistance in high-risk contexts, to financing large-scale public investment and mobilising private capital where conditions permit. Understanding how these roles relate to one another is essential for assessing whether the system's architecture remains coherent and fit for purpose, particularly in a context of rising demands and tighter resources (Figure 1.1).

- **At the non-bankable end of the spectrum, the *United Nations Development System* (UNDS) plays a foundational role in building the ecosystem that underpins development.** UNDS activities are heavily concentrated in humanitarian assistance and social sectors. These activities are rarely bankable and often take place in highly fragile or crisis-affected contexts, yet they are indispensable for protecting lives and maintaining basic service provision. Beyond immediate delivery, UNDS activities contribute to the enabling environment (including norms, institutional capacity and human capital) without which neither public nor private investment can be sustained.
- ***Vertical funds* typically operate primarily in the high-risk, catalytic segment of the financing spectrum, focusing on global public goods and market failures that require collective action.** Their strong presence in sectors such as health, climate and biodiversity reflects mandates designed to pilot new approaches, absorb early-stage risk and demonstrate viability where incentives for private investment are weak. Some vertical funds also have a footprint in infrastructure-related areas, largely related to green investments.
- **The *concessional windows of multilateral development banks* (MDBs) occupy a pivotal position in the financing spectrum, transforming high-risk investments into scalable opportunities.** These windows are active across both social and infrastructure sectors, reflecting their dual mandate: supporting essential public investments while enabling large-scale financing in low-income and vulnerable countries. In doing so, they bridge the gap between grant-based interventions and more market-oriented forms of finance.

- **At the more bankable end of the spectrum, *MDB non-concessional arms* and *private sector arms* focus on scaling infrastructure and productive investment.** These institutions play a critical role in translating earlier risk absorption and de-risking efforts into sustained investment. However, their effectiveness depends on the functioning of the upstream parts of the financing chain, which prepare countries and projects for market-based finance.

Figure 1.1. Multilateral organisations are designed to play complementary roles, providing development finance across different contexts

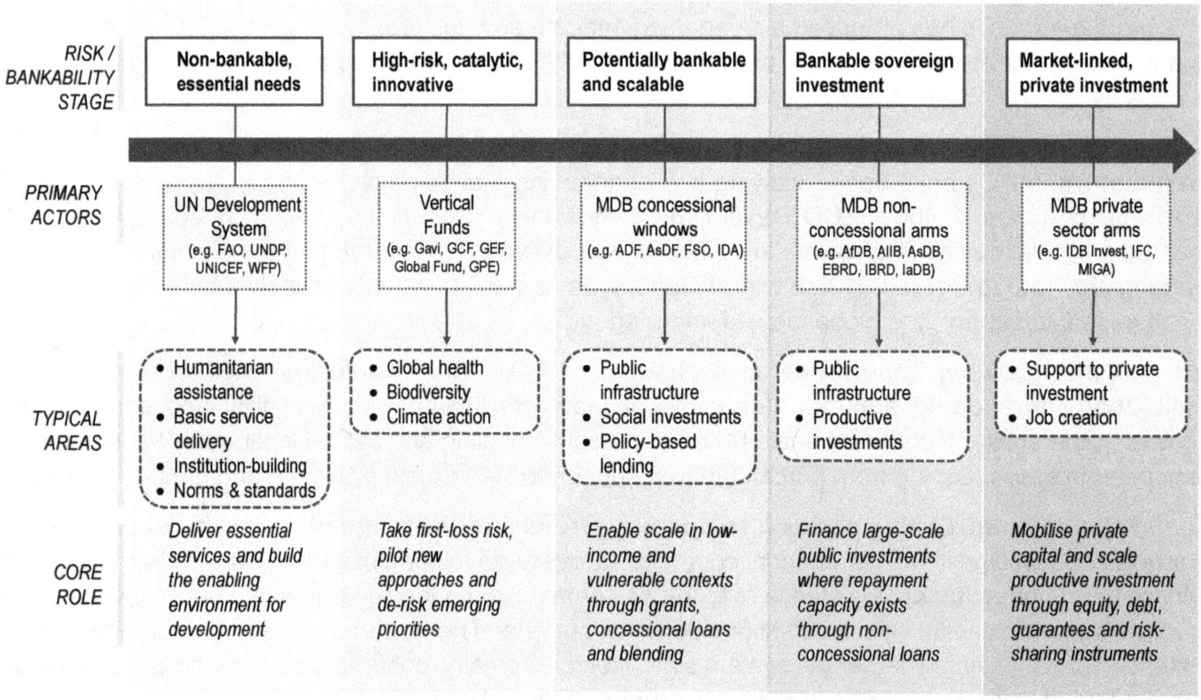

Maintaining a coherent division of labour across the multilateral development system, in a context of cuts and loss of trust, requires proactive attention from both multilateral institutions and their donors. Over time, some MDOs may expand beyond their core and traditional areas of comparative advantage in response to shifting donor priorities or competitive funding pressures. While such adaptation can be justified in specific circumstances or at the institutional level, it can also end up blurring the logical division of roles across the system. The financing spectrum presented above, although simplified and non-exhaustive, provides a broad compass for system stewardship by clarifying where each type of institution adds the greatest value.

While the multilateral development system has steadily expanded and gained new mandates over time, the conditions that enabled this growth are now changing. The multilateral development architecture, which was progressively built up in an era of relative optimism for multilateralism, now operates in a context of heightened contestation over its role, legitimacy and effectiveness, with several large donors reducing their development co-operation budgets. As a result, the system is entering a period of retrenchment, with a funding contraction estimated at about 23-30% between 2023 and 2027. These dynamics, explored in greater detail in Chapter 2, are exposing long-standing structural challenges and forcing a reassessment of the system's architecture, funding structure and strategic role.

1.1.2. Pressure on multiple fronts means the multilateral development system must adapt to survive

The multilateral development system must adapt to preserve its relevance. For years, long-standing concerns about institutional proliferation, funding quality and fragmentation have shaped debates on the effectiveness of multilateral development co-operation. However simultaneous more acute pressures are now forcing it to move from debate to action. Three inter-related forces, described below, are reshaping incentives and funding models: (i) geopolitical fragmentation and declining trust in multilateralism, (ii) tighter and more volatile aid budgets, and (iii) growing scrutiny of value for money.

The rise of a more fragmented geopolitical order could mark the end of a golden age of multilateralism

Geopolitical fragmentation is weakening the foundations of consensus-based multilateral co-operation and reshaping donor incentives. As trust among key stakeholders declines, funding and engagement decisions are increasingly influenced by national strategic considerations rather than assessments of collective efficiency or global needs.

The multilateral development system was initially designed to function as a collective investment, supported by predictable and flexible funding that enabled resource pooling and economies of scale, as illustrated by the green quadrant in Figure 1.2. Over time, however, the behaviour of multilateral stakeholders has gradually shifted: donors have progressively favoured more discretionary and earmarked forms of engagement to maximise control and visibility over their contributions, while MDOs faced incentives to expand their mandates and resources.

The current context of geopolitical fragmentation and declining trust in multilateralism is accelerating these trends, incentivising unilateral approaches and weakening the political foundations on which collective action depends. In this environment, the incentives facing both donors and multilateral development organisations increasingly resemble a prisoner's dilemma, where rational individual decisions can yield sub-optimal collective outcomes: some donors have started reducing or rebalancing their multilateral commitments and, as a result, MDOs may increasingly compete for earmarked resources to compensate for declining contributions, reinforcing behaviours that risk undermining multilateral effectiveness. These trends suggest that the system is no longer operating in the co-operative equilibrium. Instead, it increasingly resembles the intermediary and unstable configurations represented by the orange quadrants.

If these non-co-operative dynamics persist, the multilateral development system could see its foundations weaken and its effectiveness decline. If the system is allowed to drift towards a low co-operation equilibrium (red quadrant), where the retrenchment of some multilateral stakeholders prompts most others to scale back as well, this could weaken the system's foundations and reduce overall effectiveness. Avoiding this trajectory requires deliberate choices that reinforce collective incentives rather than amplify competitive dynamics.

Figure 1.2. Donors' incentives increasingly resemble a prisoner's dilemma

	Other donors cooperate	Other donors defect
Donor A cooperates	**Payoff: High** • Burden-sharing. • Multilateral core funding remains predictable. • MDOs can plan and deliver at scale, preserving collective effectiveness. • Spillovers reduce fragility and crisis spill-back to both donor and partner countries.	**Payoff: Medium** • Donor A shoulders more of the multilateral burden amid others' cuts, creating risk of moral hazard/"free riders". • Multilateral effectiveness erodes as MDOs scale back and triage. • However, reputational benefits and strategic influence inside multilaterals persist.
Donor A defects	**Payoff: Medium** • Donor A benefits from fiscal savings and ability to prioritise domestic/bilateral goals. • Donor A free-rides on others' multilateral spending. • Systemic risk rises, and donor A forfeits influence, burden-sharing, and pooled crisis tools.	**Payoff: Low** • Widespread cuts lead to steep collective underfunding, fragmentation, and weaker global public goods (health security, humanitarian response). • MDOs downsize and crisis response falters • Long-run costs (conflict, migration crises, pandemics) increase for all.

Low-co-operation equilibrium

In recent years, these geopolitical dynamics have already begun reshaping the landscape of multilateral development co-operation. As broad-based consensus becomes harder to achieve, donors and MDOs increasingly rely on narrower, coalition-based forms of engagement to advance specific priorities. The proliferation of vertical funds and other purpose-specific mechanisms since the 2000s in part reflects this trend. In this sense, the "variable geometry" multilateralism invoked by some political leaders (Government of Canada, 2026[2]) is the intensification of a longer-term trend, now accelerated by growing contestation of multilateralism and increasingly divergent priorities among donors. The growing reliance on such "coalitions of the willing" raises questions about whether such arrangements will ultimately serve as stepping stones or stumbling blocks for the multilateral system: reinforcing progress by enabling progress where consensus is elusive or further fragmenting it by diverting attention and resources away from universal frameworks.

The global aid crisis threatens to unravel the financial foundations of multilateral development co-operation

The development co-operation landscape is entering a period of acute financial stress, after major DAC providers announced substantial reductions to their aid budgets in 2025. At least 11 members of the OECD DAC are scaling back their ODA budgets, signalling a break from the expansionary trend that characterised the multilateral development system in previous decades. This group includes several of the largest contributors to the multilateral development system, such as the United States, United Kingdom, Germany and France. As shown in Figure 1.3, these members account for a substantial share of funding to major MDOs, suggesting that the impact of the announced cuts is likely to be both substantial and widespread. And as highlighted in Section 1.2.1 below, this is likely to be a sustained contraction rather than a short-lived adjustment.

Figure 1.3. The eleven DAC members that have announced aid cuts account for a significant share of major MDOs' total funding

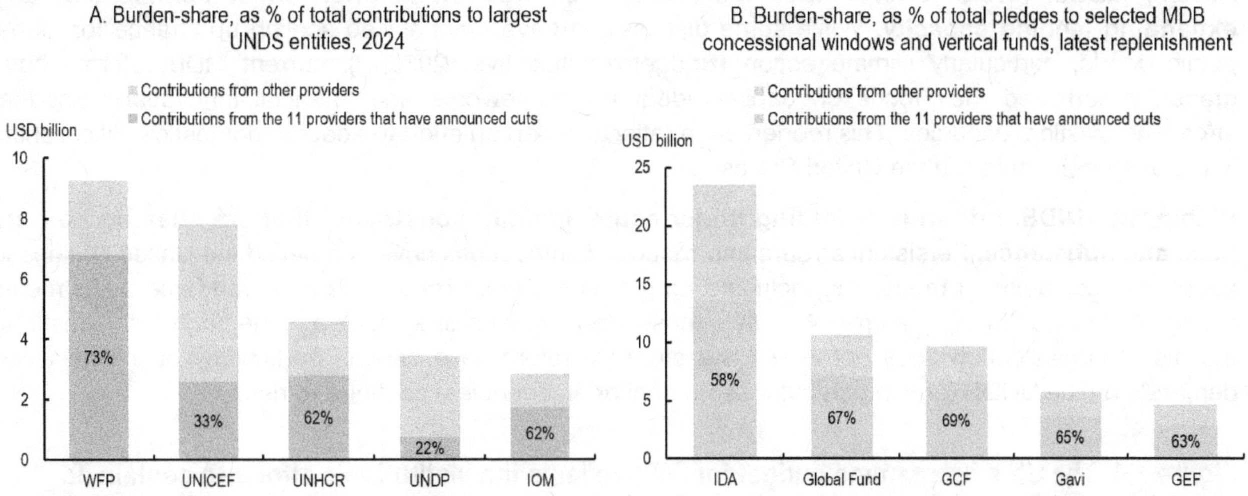

Note: Gavi=Global Alliance for Vaccines and Immunization; GCF=Green Climate Fund; GEF=Global Environment Facility; IDA=International Development Association; IOM=International Organization for Migration; UNDP=United Nations Development Programme; UNHCR= United Nations High Commissioner for Refugees; UNICEF=United Nations Children's Fund; WFP= World Food Programme.
Source: Calculations for Panel A are based on a dataset of donor contributions to the United Nations Development System (UNDS) in 2023 and 2024 provided to the authors directly by United Nations Department of Economic and Social Affairs (UNDESA). It excludes local contributions (i.e. funding provided by a government to UN activities implemented in its own country) from analysis. Calculations for Panel B are based on multilateral funds' last completed replenishments for which full contributions data is available: IDA20 (IDA, 2022[3]), Global Fund-7 (The Global Fund, 2022[4]), GCF Second Formal Replenishment (Green Climate Fund, 2023[5]), Gavi 2021-2025 (Global Alliance for Vaccines and Immunization, 2026[6]) and GEF-8 (Global Environmental Fund, 2022[7]). Not all ODA providers that have announced cuts to ODA for 2025-27 participate in all multilateral funds analysed.

StatLink https://stat.link/qdeaks

Although the most visible effects of the aid crisis have so far manifested themselves in bilateral flows, the multilateral development system is not insulated from these shocks. Reductions in bilateral aid budgets, the downsizing of development co-operation agencies, and the merging of aid portfolios into ministries of foreign affairs have made the headlines. However, signs of strains are also emerging across MDOs as funding becomes more volatile and uncertain, and a sustained reduction in funding to the multilateral development system is expected in coming years.

The extent to which these pressures translate into reduced multilateral funding will depend on how donors allocate cuts between bilateral and multilateral channels. Reductions may be transmitted symmetrically across both, fall disproportionately on multilateral contributions, or be partly offset if donors shift a larger share of constrained aid budgets through multilateral mechanisms.

Cost efficiency considerations are driving multilateral reform

Political and financial imperatives are driving multilateral reform in ways that risk sidelining effectiveness goals. In a context of tightening budgets and increased domestic accountability demands, current reform agendas are often being framed around demonstrating value for money, maximising leverage and containing costs. The current wave of multilateral reforms reflects these pressures. It includes the shareholder-driven and G7- and G20-backed efforts to expand the lending capacity of MDBs by optimising their balance sheets (U.S. Department of the Treasury, 2024[8]; G20, 2024[9]), as well as ongoing reforms within the UN system reforms aimed at improving its financial sustainability and efficiency. While these objectives respond to legitimate constraints, they can narrow the reform lens to financial metrics and short-term efficiencies, potentially sidelining more ambitious and harder-to-attain goals related to effectiveness, co-ordination and long-term development impact.

Among MDBs, reform efforts have increasingly centred on balance sheet optimisation and expanding lending capacity. While some discussions have emphasised scaling up finance for global public goods, particularly climate action (Bridgetown Initiative, 2022[10]), current MDB reforms have gradually narrowed their focus on capital adequacy frameworks and financial innovation aimed at stretching existing resources. This reorientation reflects in part an effort to adapt to domestic political shifts in major shareholders like the United States.

Within the UNDS, reform is unfolding under acute liquidity constraints that are shaping both its pace and substance. Persistent arrears and reduced contributions have compelled the United Nations to adopt cost-containment measures, including programme budget reductions and workforce adjustments (United Nations, 2025[11]) (Figure 1.4). While these steps may be unavoidable in the short term, ensuring that fiscal consolidation does not crowd out strategic reform is essential, particularly at a time when demands on the UNDS (and in particular its humanitarian agencies) continue to rise.

Figure 1.4. The UN's programme budget for 2026 reflects the institution's efforts to contain its costs

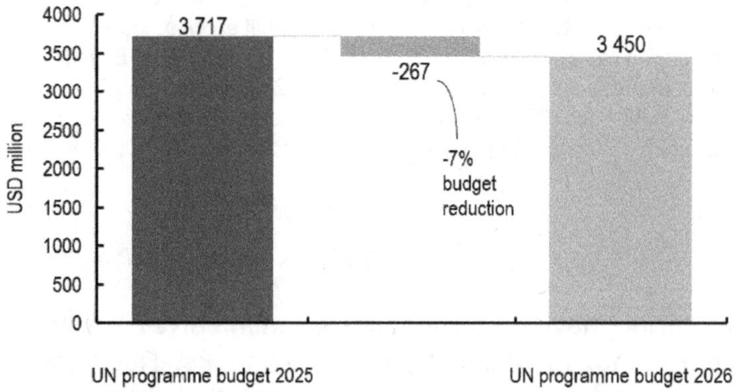

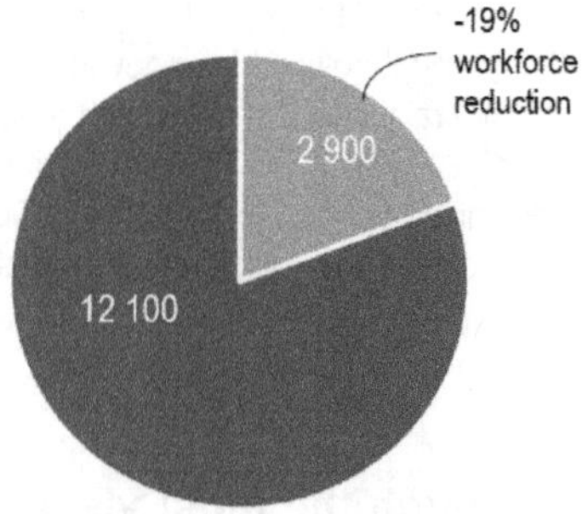

Note: The UN programme budget is used primarily to finance the operating, staff, and programme expenses of the UN's main organs (General Assembly, Security Council, Economic and Social Council, Secretariat and International Court of Justice).
Source: Authors' calculations based on United Nations (2024[12]), *Resolutions Adopted by the General Assembly on 24 December 2024*, https://digitallibrary.un.org/record/4071044?ln=en&v=pdf and United Nations (2025[13]), *Resolutions Adopted by the General Assembly on 30 December 2025*, https://docs.un.org/en/A/RES/80/244%20A-C.

StatLink https://stat.link/ybrlw1

While driven largely by political and financial imperatives, the current wave of reforms creates openings to address some long-standing structural weaknesses in the system. Persistent concerns about mandate overlap, institutional proliferation and limited transparency on system-wide results may now receive greater attention as financial pressures force clearer prioritisation. Evidence of overlapping portfolios, particularly in areas such as health, underscores the importance of clearer role differentiation and stronger co-ordination mechanisms (Sands, 2025[14]). If approached strategically, ongoing reforms could therefore strengthen systemic coherence rather than merely reduce costs. Building on and expanding the analytical work already undertaken by the OECD on portfolio similarity analysis could support this objective by clarifying the division of labour, overlaps and potential synergies across MDOs' portfolios (OECD, 2022[15]).

The three pressure points outlined in this section expose a multilateral development system that delivers significant collective value but from increasingly fragile foundations. Its ability to pool resources, leverage capital and operate across a wide range of risk and financing contexts has allowed it to achieve outcomes that the sum of individual donors could not deliver. Yet this collective value depends critically on trust in collective action and funding choices that reinforce system-wide coherence.

1.2. After years of expansion, funding to the multilateral development system has reached a turning point

1.2.1. The growth in donors' multilateral contributions has reversed, and structural challenges are now visible

After several years of sustained growth, funding to the multilateral development system reversed course in 2024, signalling a turning point in its trajectory. DAC countries' core and earmarked contributions to multilateral development organisations rose steadily through 2023, reaching a peak of USD 107.6 billion before falling to USD 91.3 billion in 2024. This represents a decline of more than 15% in real terms (Figure 1.5).

Figure 1.5. Core and earmarked contributions to the multilateral system declined by 15% in 2024

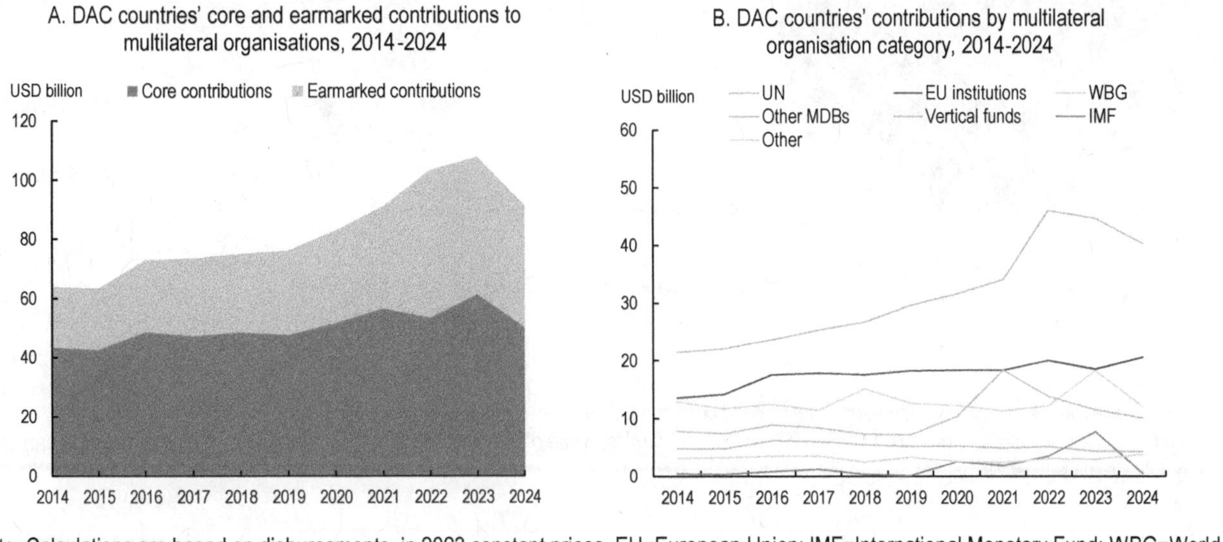

Note: Calculations are based on disbursements, in 2023 constant prices. EU=European Union; IMF=International Monetary Fund; WBG=World Bank Group.

Source: Authors' calculations based on OECD (2026[16]), *Providers' total use of the multilateral system* (database). Retrieved 22 February 2026, http://data-explorer.oecd.org/s/1td.

StatLink https://stat.link/cuwvq7

Unlike previous episodes of volatility, the 2024 decline reflects deeper structural pressures on aid budgets. Earlier fluctuations, such as the dip in core contributions in 2022, occurred within an overall upward trend and partly reflected post-crisis corrections following exceptional increases linked to the COVID-19 pandemic and Russia's war of aggression against Ukraine. By contrast, the current downturn coincides with multi-year reductions in ODA announced across several major donors, suggesting that the contraction in multilateral contributions signals a medium-term reversal rather than a temporary adjustment.

The system's heavy reliance on a few DAC donors leaves it highly exposed to cuts

The concentration of multilateral funding among a small number of DAC donors amplifies the system's exposure to the announced cuts. As mentioned above, a large share of DAC members' contributions to the multilateral development system comes from donors that have announced aid cuts. Eleven DAC members, collectively accounting for 63% of total DAC contributions to the system in 2024, have announced reductions to their ODA budgets in 2024 (Figure 1.3 and Figure 1.6), with most anticipating further cuts through the end of 2027 (OECD, 2025[17]). The simultaneous and substantial funding cuts by one third of the DAC membership are unprecedented in recent decades, and have system-wide implications.

Figure 1.6. The 11 DAC members that have publicly announced cuts in their ODA in 2025-27 accounted for roughly two-thirds of total DAC contributions to the system in 2024

Share of DAC members' total contributions, 2024

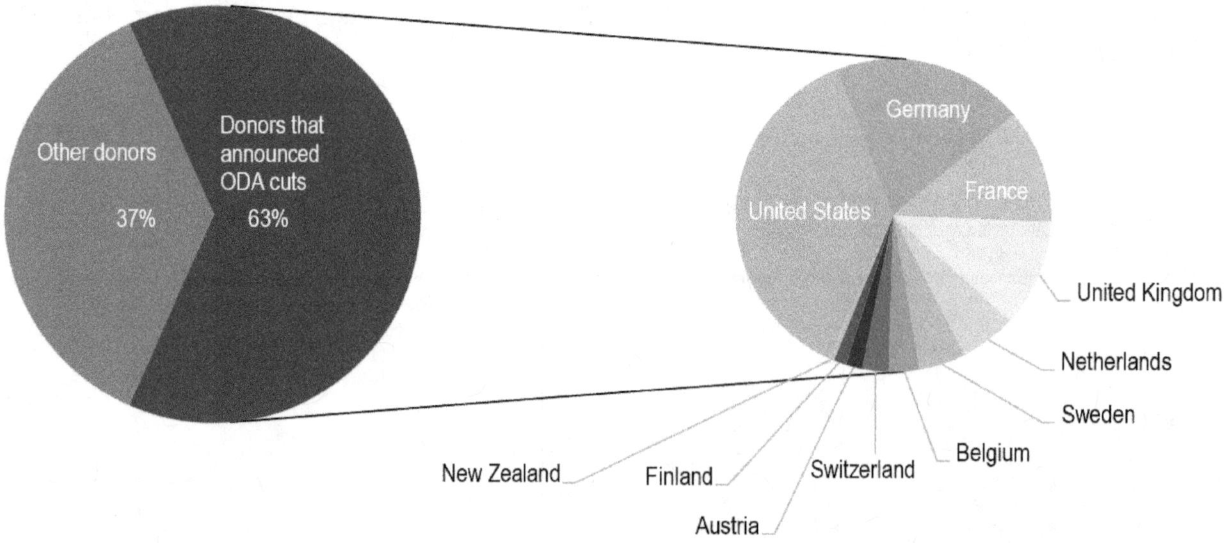

Note: Calculations are based on disbursements, in 2023 constant prices.
Source: Authors' calculations based on OECD (2026[16]), *Providers' total use of the multilateral system* (database). Retrieved 22 February 2026, http://data-explorer.oecd.org/s/1td.

StatLink https://stat.link/raj04t

Forward-looking projections suggest that multilateral contributions could decline further if the announced aid cuts are implemented as planned. Based on survey data on expected changes in DAC members' ODA budgets (OECD, 2025[17]), total funding to the multilateral development system could fall by between approximately 23% and 30% between 2023 and 2027 (Figure 1.7), reinforcing the likelihood of a sustained contraction rather than a short-lived adjustment.

Figure 1.7. Contributions to the multilateral development system are set to continue declining

DAC members' total contributions to the multilateral system, 2010-2024 and projections

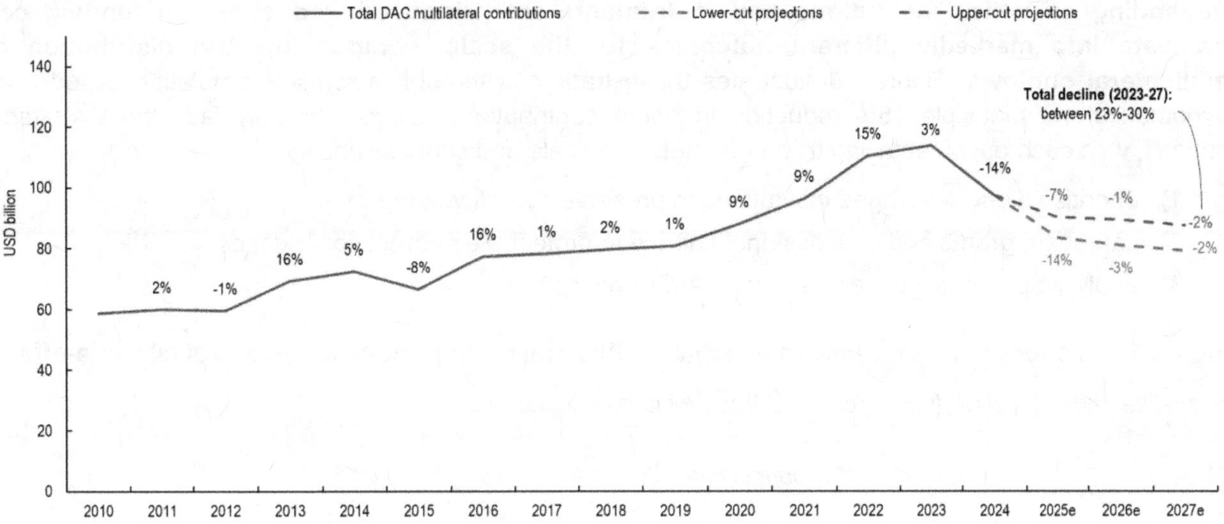

Note: Calculations are based on disbursements, in 2023 constant prices. Projections are generated by applying each donor's ODA percentage change, as estimated in (OECD, 2025[17]), to their respective multilateral contributions.

Source: Authors' calculations based on OECD (2026[16]), OECD Data Explorer, *Providers' total use of the multilateral system* (database). Retrieved 22 February 2026, http://data-explorer.oecd.org/s/1td and OECD (2025[17]), *Cuts in official development assistance: OECD projections for 2025 and the near term*, https://doi.org/10.1787/8c530629-en.

StatLink https://stat.link/nrgd9f

The pullback by the multilateral system's traditional donors could accelerate changes in donor patterns and influence. Although non-DAC government donors and private providers remain relatively small contributors at the system level, targeted increases can materially affect individual organisations' financing structures and governance dynamics when major donors scale back.

The latest replenishments of the International Development Association (IDA), the World Bank Group's concessional window, is a case in point. During IDA21, concluded in 2025, several top donors (United States, Japan, Germany and France) reduced their pledges compared to the previous cycle. The People's Republic of China, hereafter China, meanwhile, boosted its pledge by 14%, becoming a top five pledger to an IDA replenishment for the first time in history. This is a notable rise considering China ranked only 20th as recently as IDA16, concluded in 2010 (Martinez and Estes, 2025[18]).

Similar dynamics are visible among private donors, which can assume greater prominence when traditional providers scale back. For example, in the absence of a United States pledge in the latest GAVI replenishment, the Gates Foundation became the institution's second largest contributor, behind the United Kingdom (Rigby, 2025[19]), and the largest funder of the World Health Organisation's (WHO) core budget. This has left the philanthropic organisations with an extraordinarily large donor share and influence over global public health governance.

1.2.2. What the funding dry-out means for the multilateral development system

Shrinking funding raises difficult trade-offs for donors to the multilateral development system

Depending on which institutions and instruments are prioritised, reductions in funding can translate into markedly different outcomes for the scale, composition and distribution of multilateral outflows. Figure 1.8 illustrates these trade-offs through a stylised simulation based on a hypothetical yet plausible 15% reduction in donor contributions. Donors broadly face three strategic options, with each option entailing trade-offs between scale and concessionality:

1) prioritise highly leveraged institutions to preserve overall volumes;
2) safeguard grants and concessional finance to protect the poorest contexts; or
3) apply proportional cuts across the board ("haircut").

Figure 1.8. Donor choices on how to allocate multilateral contributions involve explicit trade-offs

Illustrative trade-offs of aid funding cuts: 15% budget cuts scenario

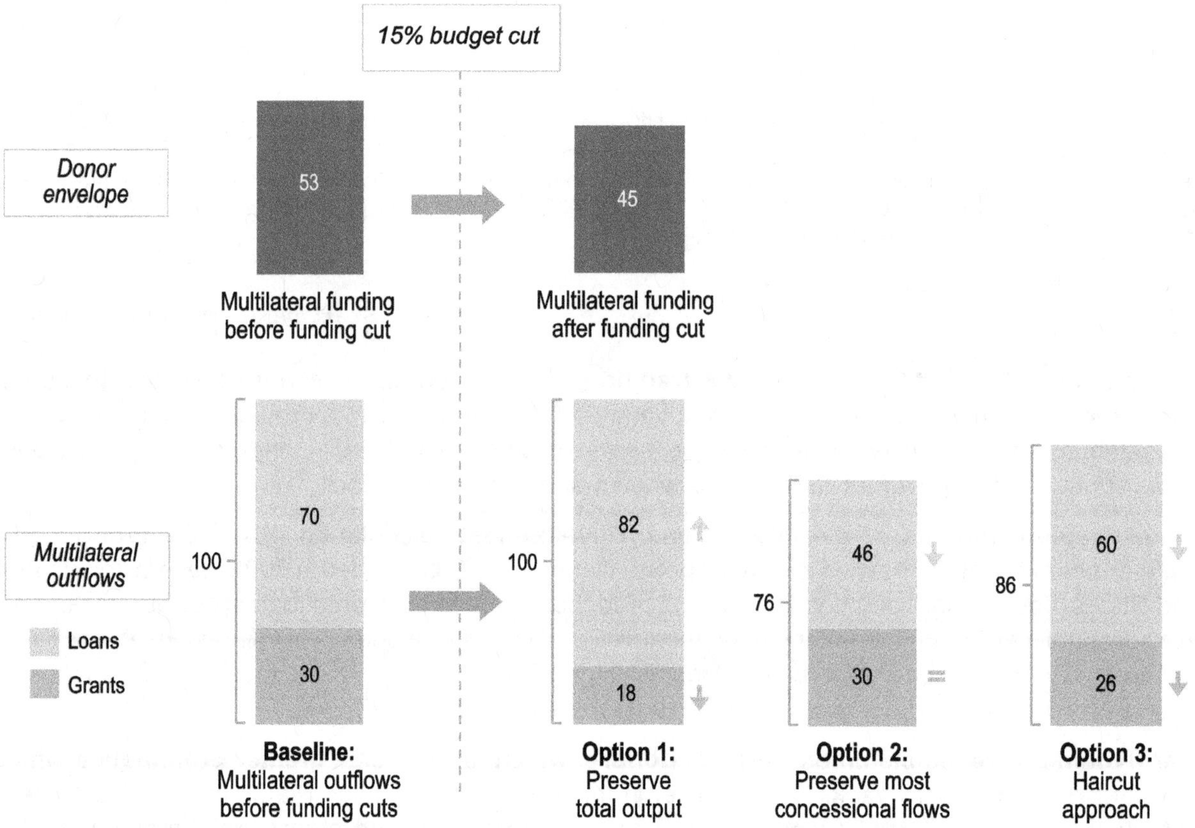

Note: To keep the illustration transparent, the simulation assumes simplified leverage relationships: grant financing is treated as having a one-to-one relationship between donor cost and financing delivered, while loans are assumed to generate three dollars of financing for each dollar of donor contribution. The baseline scenario assumes an outflow composition of 30% grants and 70% loans, which broadly represents the historical balance between concessional and non-concessional multilateral finance.

These three scenarios illustrate why the frequently invoked ambition for the multilateral development system to "do more with less" is unrealistic in a contracting funding environment. While multilateral development organisations can sometimes increase productivity and efficiency through reforms or innovation, evidence from recent and ongoing reforms shows that such gains take time to materialise and do not eliminate the need for trade-offs (G20 Independent Experts Group, 2024[20]; Dag Hammarskjöld Foundation, 2021[21]). When overall donor envelopes shrink significantly, multilateral stakeholders cannot simultaneously preserve volumes and concessionality. The question facing donors is therefore not whether the system can absorb cuts without consequences, but which objectives should be prioritised and which consequences they are willing to accept.

Shifts in core and earmarked funding could compound the effects of declining multilateral contributions

The balance between core and earmarked contributions has major implications for how the system functions. Core contributions provide MDOs with flexibility to deliver on their mandates, invest in institutional capacities, and respond to evolving needs within an overarching strategy. Non-core, earmarked contributions allow member states to retain a degree of control over their use and can help target emerging priorities. When used strategically and aligned with institutional mandates and partner country priorities, earmarking can therefore play a constructive role in the system. However, extensive reliance on earmarked funding has also been shown to fragment funding, increase transaction costs, and reduce multilateral flexibility (Ihl et al., 2025[22]). Changes to this balance therefore affect not only individual organisations, but also the coherence of the multilateral development system as a whole.

Earmarked funding has risen steadily over the past decade and may increasingly displace core multilateral funding as budgets tighten. Figure 1.9 shows that its share of DAC members' total ODA increased from 11% in 2010 to 18% in 2024, peaking at 21% in 2022. Over the same period, core multilateral funding, which had remained close to 27% for most of the past decade, fell to 23% in 2024, signalling that core funding can become a margin of adjustment when priorities shift and donor envelopes contract.

Figure 1.9. Core multilateral contributions are being squeezed by rising bilateral and earmarked multilateral allocations

Share of DAC countries' direct bilateral, core and earmarked multilateral contributions in total ODA, 2010-2024

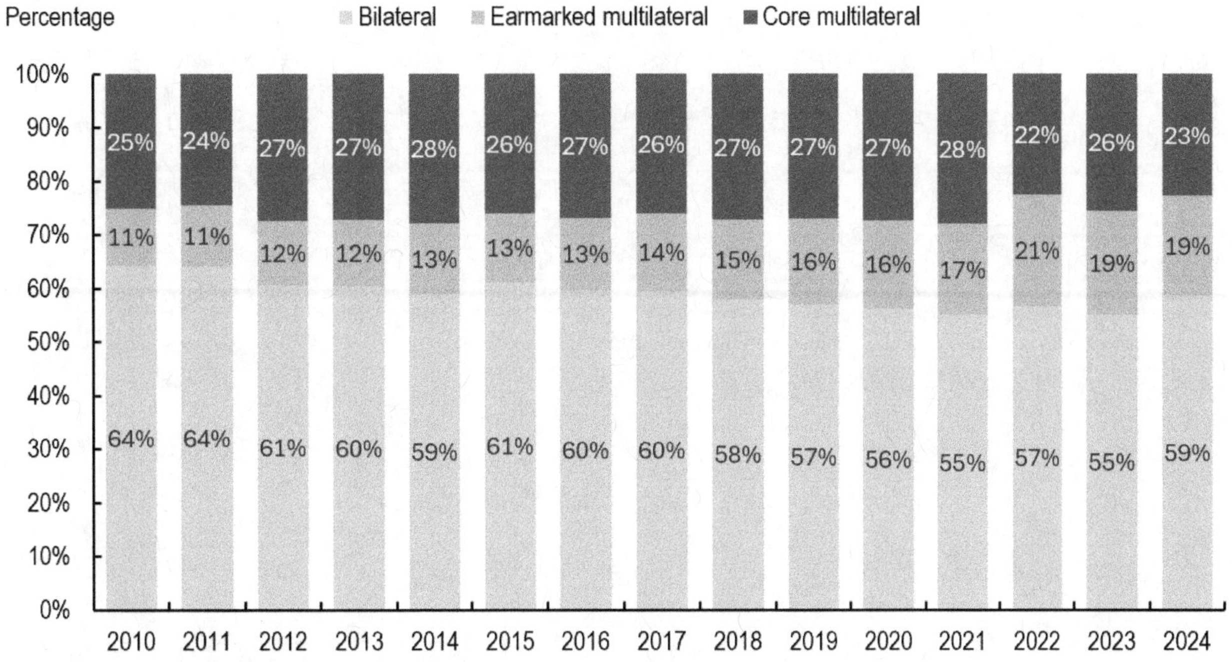

Note: Direct bilateral ODA refers to DAC members' bilateral ODA excluding earmarked contributions (multi-bi aid). Calculations are based on gross disbursements in 2023 constant prices.
Source: Authors' calculations based on OECD (2026[23]), DAC1: Flows by provider (ODA+OOF+Private) (dataset). Retrieved 22 February 2026, http://data-explorer.oecd.org/s/9w.

StatLink https://stat.link/ncpl0o

A shift from earmarking displacing bilateral programmes to earmarking displacing core funding would weaken multilateral effectiveness. Without sufficient core resources, multilateral development organisations may struggle to finance cross-cutting functions such as country co-ordination or rapid responses to emerging crises that cannot be easily financed through tightly earmarked projects. Moreover, when earmarking displaces core funding, multilateralism risks becoming a channel for bilateral priorities rather than a platform for collective action. Preserving core funding is therefore not only a question of institutional stability, but also of restoring the system's founding logic.

Individual multilateral development organisations vary in their exposure and vulnerability to donor cuts

Funding reductions and shifts in funding modalities, such as a move from flexible to more tightly earmarked contributions, do not affect all multilateral development organisations equally. The impact of donor cuts on individual organisations depends not only on the size of cuts, but also on structural characteristics of the organisations themselves. These characteristics include their funding model (grant-based versus leveraged), the concentration of their donor base, their reliance on voluntary versus assessed contributions, and their access to private sources of finance. Rather than representing isolated risks, these dimensions often interact, amplifying the exposure of individual organisations to funding cuts and donor withdrawals.

Across the UNDS, multiple dimensions of funding vulnerability often coincide, creating particularly high exposure to funding contractions. Figure 1.10 illustrates how most UNDS entities rely overwhelmingly on voluntary funding, draw funding from a relatively concentrated group of government donors, and attract limited private resources. Organisations that combine these three factors (such as IOM, WFP, UNAIDS and UNODC) emerge as particularly exposed to reductions in multilateral contributions (top-right quadrant).

Figure 1.10. Most UNDS entities exhibit a high reliance on voluntary contributions

Share of voluntary funding (%), government donor concentration (0-100) and share of private funding of UNDS entities, 2023-2024 average

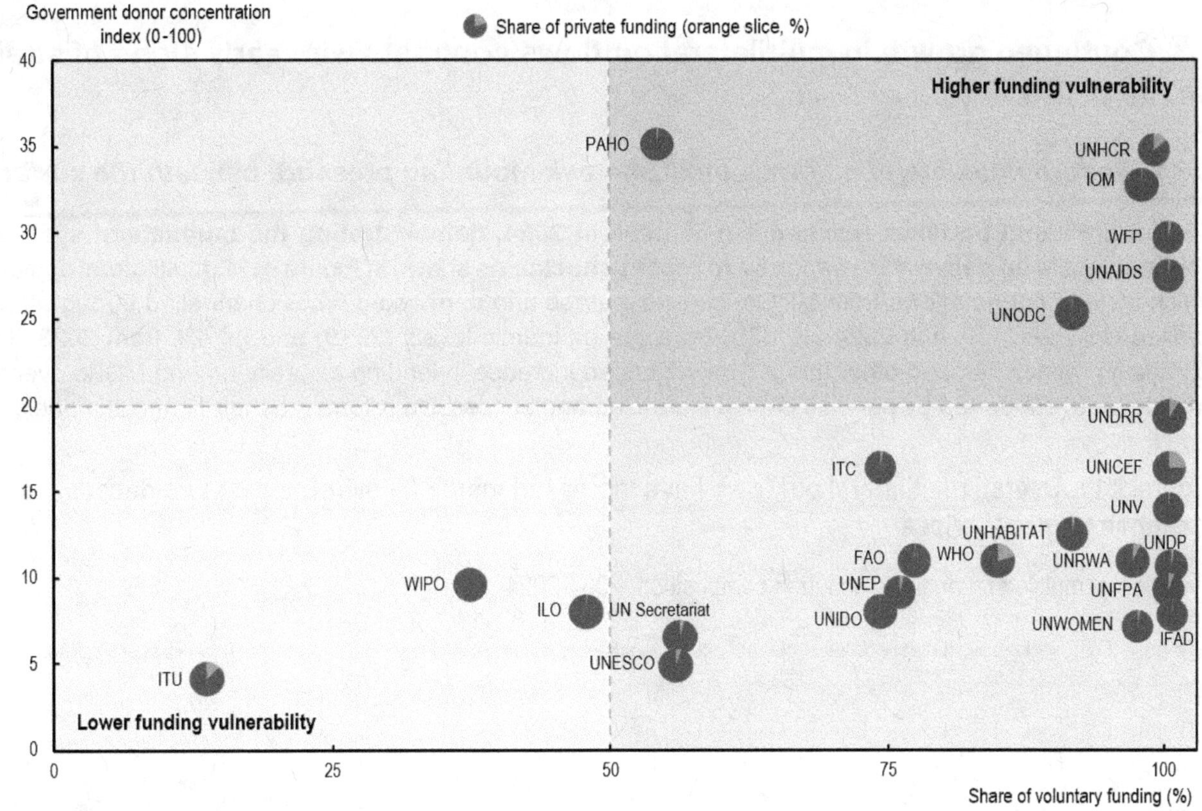

Note: The share of voluntary funding (x-axis) ranges from 0% (only assessed funding) to 100% (only voluntary funding). The government donor concentration index (y-axis) captures whether each organisation's funding from official bilateral donors is evenly distributed amongst all government donors (0) or whether it is concentrated amongst just a few (100). The share of private funding (%) represents the proportion of funding from the private sector, foundations and NGOs in total funding. The chart includes all entities in the UNDS except those with 10 or fewer government donors both in 2023 and 2024. The chart excludes local contributions from the analysis (i.e. funding provided by a government to UN activities implemented in its own country).

Source: Authors' calculations based on a dataset of donor contributions to the United Nations Development System (UNDS) in 2024 provided to the authors directly by United Nations Department of Economic and Social Affairs (UNDESA).

StatLink https://stat.link/krj31h

The experience of UNESCO illustrates the risks of funding volatility, but also the scope for organisational adaptation. Repeated funding suspensions and withdrawals by the United States since 2011 have exposed the organisation to significant funding shocks. Following the 2017 US withdrawal, increased voluntary contributions from other members helped cushion the impact in the short term. Beyond these short-term adjustments, UNESCO is pursuing various longer-term adaptation strategies. These include efforts to further diversify its donor base, adjust expenditures, and continue reforms already underway. Although the organisation has also engaged in risk anticipation and mitigation to soften the impact of the most recent withdrawal by the United States, the latter is still expected to have material financial and operational effects, highlighting both the opportunities and limits of organisational adaptation to funding volatility.

How multilateral development organisations respond to these funding pressures will shape not only the volume and composition of multilateral resources, but also how effectively they are able to deploy them. The next section examines multilateral outflows, analysing how multilateral development organisations translate contributions into financing for low- and middle-income countries.

1.3. Continued growth in multilateral outflows contrasts with early signs of strain on the UNDS

1.3.1. Record multilateral outflows in 2024 mask mounting pressure beneath the surface

Total multilateral outflows reached a new peak in 2024, demonstrating the multilateral system's ability to scale up delivery in response to recent shocks. As shown in Figure 1.11, multilateral outflows, which include both outflows from MDOs' core resources and earmarked flows channelled through them, totalled USD 296 billion in 2024, up 37% from pre-pandemic levels (2019) and up 4% from 2023. This expansion reflects, among other things, the sustained increase in lending capacity among MDBs over the past decade, supported by periodic capital increases and successive reforms to their financial models.

Figure 1.11. Overall multilateral outflows have increased markedly over the past two decades in response to global crises

Evolution of multilateral outflows and their composition, 2004-2024

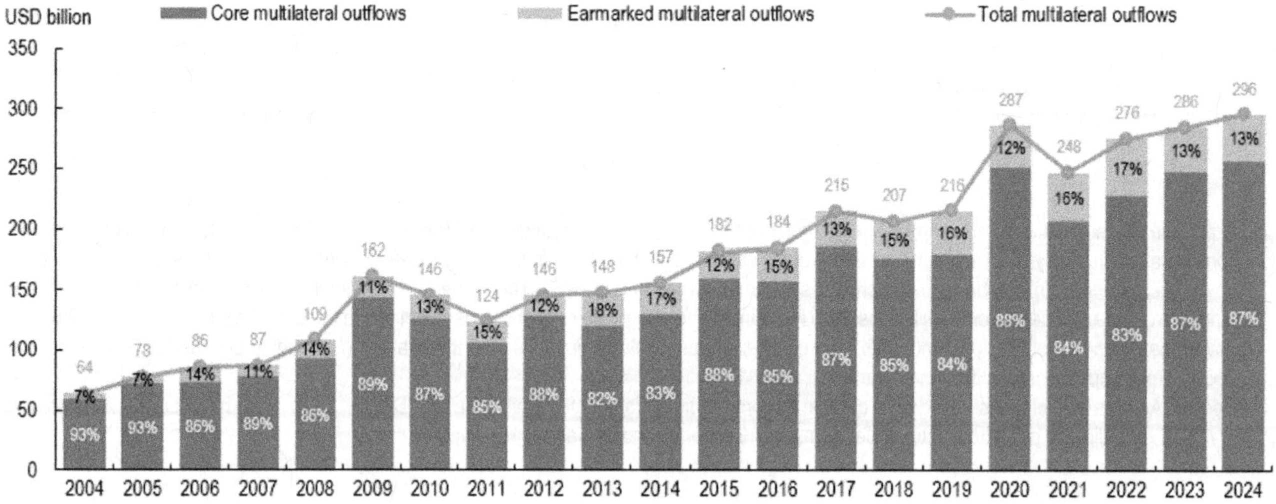

Note: Calculations are based on commitments, in 2023 constant prices. Calculations include ODA loans, ODA grants, other official flows (OOF) (excluding export credits), equity investments, and private sector instruments (PSIs).
Source: Authors' calculations based on OECD (2026[24]), *Creditor Reporting System* (dataset). Retrieved 22 February 2026, https://data-explorer.oecd.org/s/52.

StatLink https://stat.link/48jnqt

However, this apparent resilience reflects cushioning mechanisms that may delay, but not prevent, adjustment. Because parts of the system operate through multi-year arrangements (e.g. replenishments) and, in the case of MDBs, through balance sheet models, there may be a lag between deteriorating inflow conditions and multilateral outflows contractions. While these features can temporarily cushion delivery and delay funding cuts, they also risk obscuring the extent of the underlying strain on the multilateral development system and delay necessary adjustments. Once this buffer is exhausted, however, multilateral institutions may need to scale back existing or new commitments, increasing the risk of a sharper downturn in multilateral outflows than current headline figures suggest.

Early signs of strain are appearing, particularly among grant-based UNDS entities

While MDBs have continued expanding lending volumes, many UNDS entities have experienced a stagnation or decline in their outflows since 2022. The contraction is particularly pronounced among large humanitarian UNDS entities. Between 2022 and 2024, outflows from the World Food Programme (WFP), the largest UNDS agency by volume of financing delivered, fell by nearly one-third (-31%), from USD 8.2 billion to USD 5.6 billion (Figure 1.12). The humanitarian implications are immediate and far-reaching. In early 2025, WFP forecast that a further 34% funding cut relative to 2024 could materialise (WFP, 2025[25]). Under that scenario, 16.7 million people, representing around 21% of its beneficiaries, would lose access to food assistance.

Figure 1.12. Major UNDS organisations are already experiencing a significant drop in their outflows

Change in outflow volume among top 20 UNDS organisations, 2022-2024

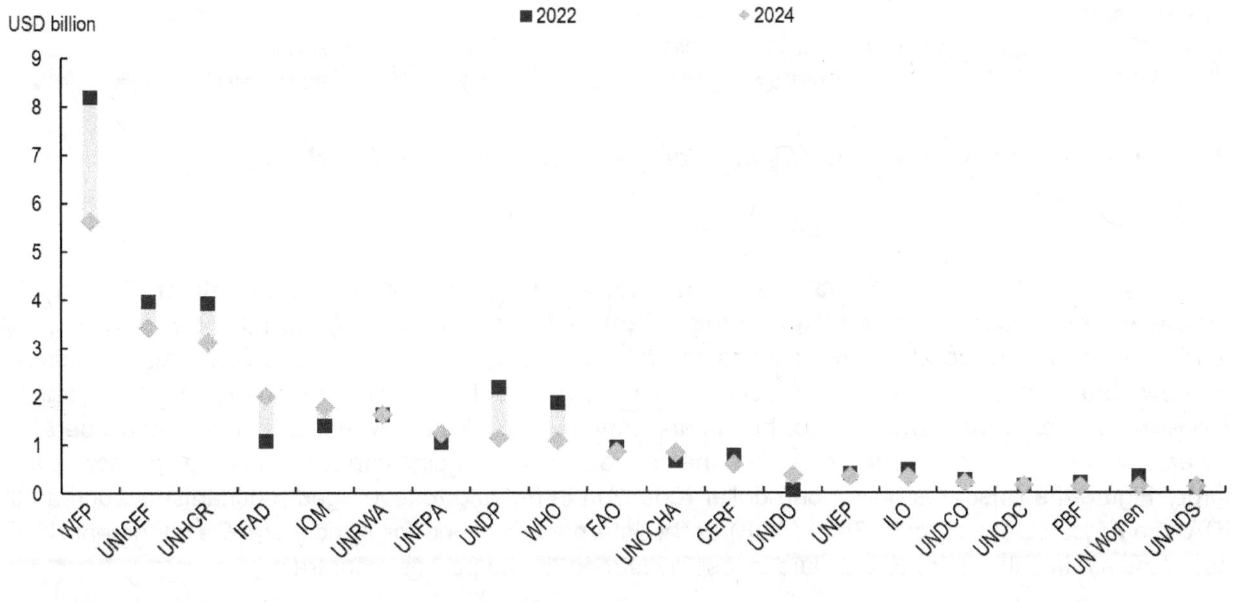

Note: Calculations are based on commitments, in 2023 constant prices.
Source: Authors' calculations based on OECD (2026[24]), *Creditor Reporting System* (dataset). Retrieved 22 February 2026, https://data-explorer.oecd.org/s/52.

StatLink https://stat.link/me92kl

In the short term, many multilateral development organisations are resorting to adjustment measures to absorb the funding shock. Across the system, MDOs have introduced hiring freezes, expenditure deferrals and administrative cost containment. Evidence from a recent survey of MDOs also indicates that funding cuts are already leading to programme delays, reduced geographic coverage and lower delivery targets (Figure 1.13). In addition, funding cuts are placing pressure on upstream functions that are less visible but critical to development effectiveness, such as policy support, oversight and norm-setting.

Figure 1.13. More than 70% of survey respondents anticipate scaling back or suspending projects due to funding cuts

Operational implications of current funding reductions to MDOs

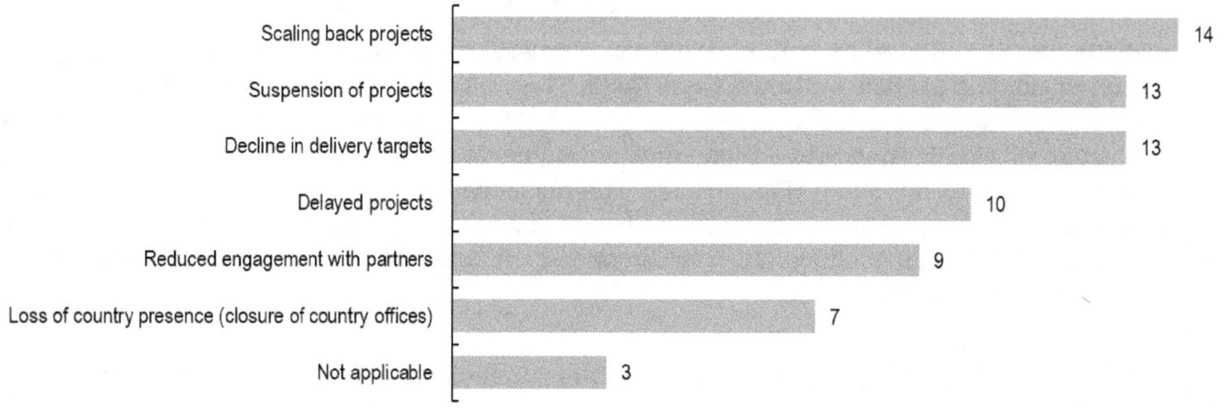

Note: This graph presents the survey respondents' responses to the question "What are the operational implications of the current funding reductions for your organisation?". The 18 survey respondents included 14 UN entities, three partnerships or funds and one international financial institution.
Source: MOPAN (2025[26]), *Mapping of Multilateral Organisations' Response to the Current Funding Environment*, https://www.mopan.org/content/dam/mopan/en/publications/our-work/insights/thematic-briefs/mapping/mopan-mapping-exercise-2025.pdf.

1.3.2. The coming squeeze raises implications for multilateral outflows

Impacts on the system's reach and ambition may be substantial and lasting

The very strengths that have enabled the multilateral development system to deliver at scale also create vulnerabilities in times of tightening aid budgets. In normal times, institutions with the capacity to leverage members' contributions, such as multilateral development banks and replenished concessional windows multiply each dollar of donor support into several dollars of financing, allowing the system to mobilise resources far beyond direct budgetary contributions. Yet, this multiplier effect can operate in reverse: when donor commitments decline, the contraction in financing capacity can be disproportionately large. Figure 4.9 illustrates how a one-dollar reduction in funding to leveraged mechanisms such as the IDA, the African Development Fund (ADF) or the International Fund for Agricultural Development (IFAD) can translate into three or more dollars in lost investment in the poorest countries.

Figure 1.14. Defunding multilateral leveraged mechanisms risks generating outflow losses that far exceed the budgetary savings achieved

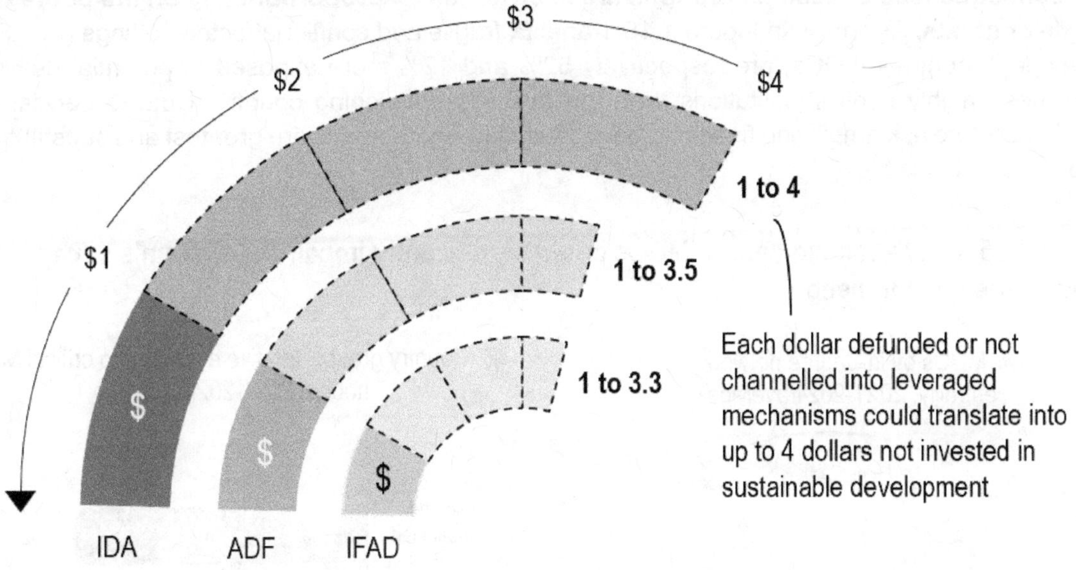

Source: IFAD (2025[27]), *2025 Report on IFAD's Development Effectiveness*, https://webapps.ifad.org/members/eb/145/docs/english/EB-2025-145-R-19.pdf?attach=1; African Development Bank (2025[28]), "African Development Fund mobilises a historic $11 billion, marking a new era of African ownership and investment-led development", https://www.afdb.org/en/news-and-events/press-releases/african-development-fund-mobilises-historic-11-billion-marking-new-era-african-ownership-and-investment-led-development-89755; World Bank Group (2023[29]), IDA20 Mid-term Review, https://thedocs.worldbank.org/en/doc/f1d0b477064fadf03bd4e4aa96b5b63d-0410012023/original/ida-20-MTR-factsheet-11-16-2020.pdf.

Given these dynamics, bilateral providers must deploy scarce resources strategically to preserve the catalytic impact of the multilateral system. In other words, they should make deliberate choices about where resources can unlock the greatest development impact, without diluting mandates or exacerbating duplication. This may involve reassessing how scarce donor resources are allocated and comparing the expected development impacts of various funding modalities and mechanisms. For example, targeted core contributions to MDB concessional windows might generate greater impact than a multitude of small, fragmented contributions to MDB trust funds.

The implications of funding cuts extend beyond individual organisations to the whole system. The following section examines how cuts to some central institutions within the multilateral architecture may generate ripple effects across the system and to the countries it serves.

Uncoordinated funding cuts to central multilateral channels could trigger system-wide delivery failures

The multilateral development system functions as an interdependent delivery chain along which disruptions at central nodes can reverberate widely. Bilateral donors rely heavily on UNDS entities to implement humanitarian and development programmes. Vertical funds depend on MDBs and UNDS entities as implementing partners for green and health financing. Normative agencies, such as the WHO or ILO, shape standards and frameworks that other development actors operationalise.

In this interconnected architecture, where cuts are applied can matter as much as their scale. The network centrality analysis in Figure 1.15, Panel A indicates that several of the institutions most central to the multilateral delivery chain and therefore most relied upon by other actors – such as UNHCR, UNICEF and UN Women – are among those currently facing funding pressures. When cuts affect the highly central nodes, the risk is not only a contraction of their own operations, but also a weakening of the system's connective tissue, impacting operational continuity across the network.

The consequences of such disruptions are likely to fall disproportionately on the poorest and most fragile contexts. As shown in Figure 1.15, Panel B, fragile and conflict-affected settings (FCAS) and least developed countries (LDCs) are respectively 52% and 42% more exposed to potential delivery failures from these highly central institutions than the average developing country. Cuts to central multilateral actors therefore risk amplifying financing gaps precisely where needs are greatest and substitution by other actors is least feasible.

Figure 1.15. Cuts affecting central MDOs could significantly impair the system's capacity to support the most in need

A. MDOs by in-degree network centrality, 2021-2024 average

B. Country groups' relative exposure to critical MDO nodes, 2021-2024 average

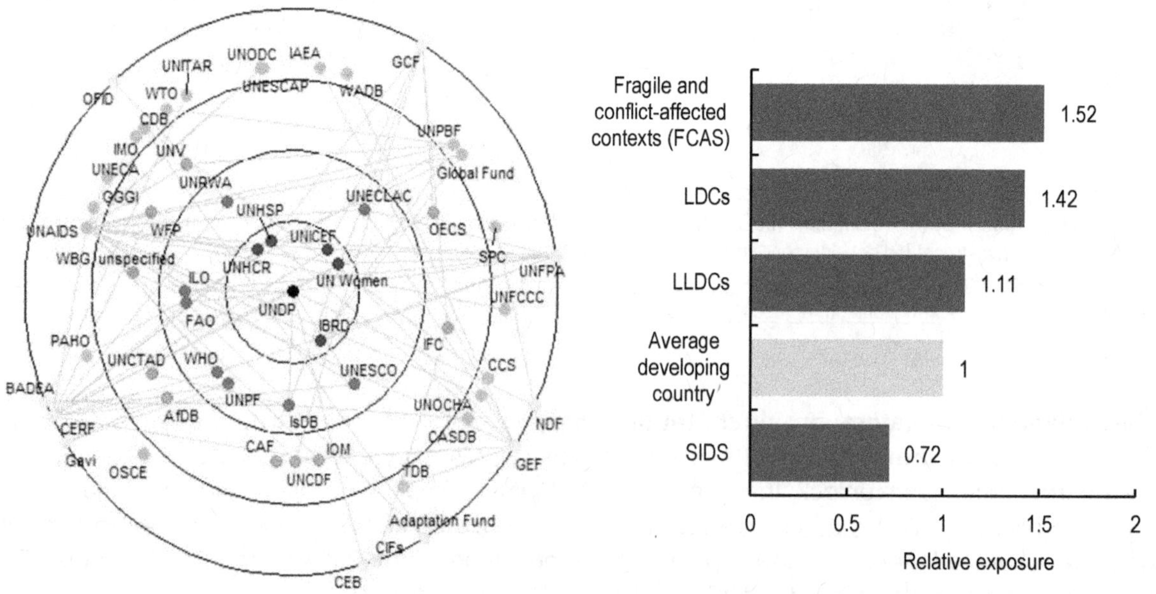

Note: In Panel A, in-degree network centrality measures how many incoming connections an organisation receives from others in the network. Applied here to the network of multilateral development organisations, it highlights which MDOs are most frequently relied upon as delivery channels within the multilateral development system. MDOs with the highest network centrality scores appear in the inner circles of the network graph and are represented in darker colours. Panel B shows the relative exposure of different country groups to potential delivery failures by MDOs that both exhibit a high in-degree centrality score and are affected by current funding reductions, namely: UNHCR, UNICEF, United Nations Human Settlements Programme (UNHSP), UNDP and UN Women.

Source: Authors' calculations based on OECD (2026[24]), *Creditor Reporting System* (dataset). Retrieved 22 February 2026, https://data-explorer.oecd.org/s/52.

StatLink https://stat.link/fjkeo7

Beyond the risk of delivery chain disruptions, the current funding environment risks shifting where and how multilateral resources are allocated. Under pressure to demonstrate scale and financial returns, institutions may prioritise operations that maximise leverage or disbursement speed, potentially at the expense of harder-to-finance contexts and sectors.

Concessional resources are at risk, with consequences for the most vulnerable

Concessional finance is central to the multilateral development system's ability to serve low-income countries and essential social sectors. In 2024, concessional flows accounted for the overwhelming majority of multilateral financing received by low-income countries, while humanitarian, governance and social sectors also relied predominantly on grants and highly concessional resources (Figure 1.16). If these instruments become the primary margin of adjustment under fiscal pressure, the consequences will fall disproportionately on countries and sectors with the least access to alternative sources of finance.

Figure 1.16. Low-income countries and social and humanitarian sectors are particularly exposed to cuts in multilateral concessional finance

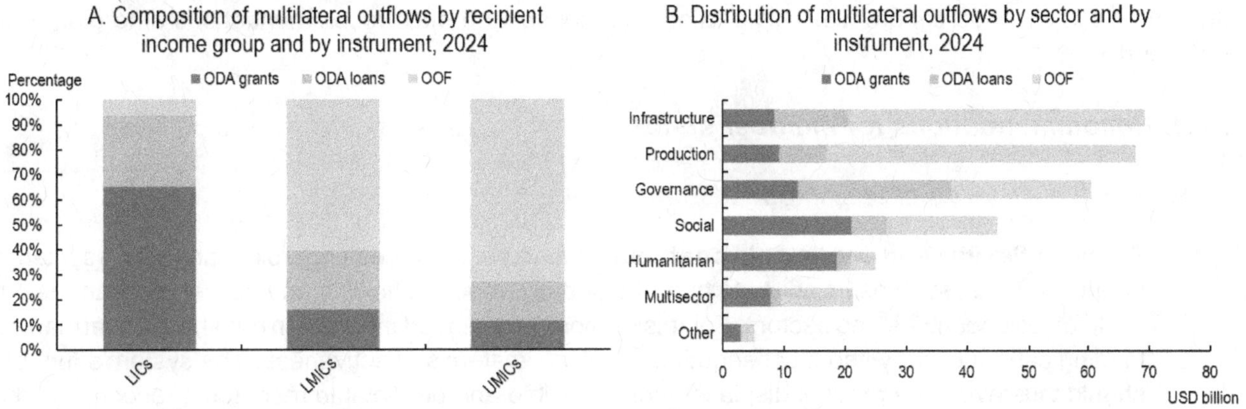

Note: Calculations are based on commitments, in 2023 constant prices. Charts illustrate volumes of ODA loans, ODA grants, and OOF (excluding export credits) but do not display equity investment and private sector instruments (PSIs), which represent marginal shares of total volumes. These components are nevertheless included in the calculations presented in the text.
LIC=low-income country; LMIC=lower-middle income country; UMIC=upper-middle income country.
Source: Authors' calculations based on OECD (2026[24]), *Creditor Reporting System* (dataset). Retrieved 22 February 2026, https://data-explorer.oecd.org/s/52.

StatLink https://stat.link/etc0r7

Declining bilateral ODA to the poorest and most vulnerable countries further increases the strategic importance of multilateral concessional finance. Recent OECD projections suggest that LDCs and sub-Saharan Africa could face double-digit declines in net bilateral ODA in 2025 compared to 2023 levels (OECD, 2025[17]). Because a substantial share of support to these contexts is also channelled through multilateral institutions, the role of the multilateral development system as a stabilising anchor becomes more pronounced when bilateral engagement contracts. If multilateral concessional finance retrenches in parallel, vulnerable countries may face compounded financing gaps.

In this context, safeguarding concessional capacity becomes a strategic imperative. Protecting allocations to low-income and fragile settings, as well as to sectors such as humanitarian action, basic services and human capital, requires deliberate prioritisation within shrinking envelopes. Without this discipline, the multilateral development system risks drifting towards easier-to-finance contexts. However, doing so requires managing a strategic tension in development finance: between deploying scarce public resources where they can mobilise the greatest volume of additional capital, and directing them to contexts where no other sources of finance are available.

Multilateral stakeholders therefore face a critical choice between unmanaged retrenchment and deliberate strategic adaptation. That choice will determine whether the system emerges from this period diminished and more fragmented, or leaner and strategically refocused around its core principle of collective action.

1.4. Stronger together: An agenda to reset the multilateral development system

Periods of constraint can create openings for renewal: the current inflection point offers an opportunity to reset the multilateral development system, based on its core original principles. The pressures facing the system need not lead to a loss of effectiveness if they are met with deliberate and co-ordinated action. Deliberate choices under constraints need to be made so that the system remains greater than the sum of its parts. Member states and multilateral development organisations share a responsibility to safeguard the system's core function: enabling collective action and delivering beyond what bilateral approaches can achieve. With deliberate and co-ordinated action by both member states and multilateral development organisations, the system can emerge leaner and more focused, retaining a capacity to deliver value that no single actor can achieve. Enhancing the system's effectiveness requires multilateral organisations to pursue reforms that sharpen rather than dilute their development additionality and strengthen system-wide coherence. This section summarises the main recommendations emerging from this report.

1.4.1. Recommendations for member states

Protect the system's financial foundations

- **Preserve flexible and predictable contributions.** Core resources underpin many of the system's unique benefits, such as its ability to operate globally, respond flexibly and deliver programmes at scale across countries and sectors. For this reason, a continued increase in the share of earmarked funding cannot occur without consequences for the system's effectiveness. The system's funders should thus avoid the gradual displacement of flexible and predictable resources, recognising the essential role of core contributions in supporting mandate delivery.
- **Use earmarked funding more strategically to restore coherence in the system.** In the near term, reducing the share of earmarking may not be realistic, particularly as such modalities can help sustain organisations financially in periods of retrenchment by major donors. Controlling for that potentially distortionary effect of earmarking is possible however, if such funding is aligned with (i) donor priorities, (ii) institutional mandates and (iii) partner country strategies. This "triple alignment" approach can help balance accountability and visibility with collective objectives. This requires donors to clarify in their multilateral engagement strategies how they intend to use different funding modalities.
- **Reassess burden-sharing among the funders of the system.** The recent contraction in multilateral contributions has exposed the heavy reliance of many multilateral development organisations on a limited number of contributors, which makes them vulnerable to policy shifts or budget cuts by a handful of member states. Diversifying the funding base can help reduce this vulnerability. Internally (within the DAC), this means avoiding excessive donor concentration that leaves organisations dependent on one or a few major DAC funders. Externally (beyond the DAC), it implies engaging emerging donors and exploring ways of increasing their participation in replenishments.

Avoid indiscriminate and uncoordinated cuts that risk generating systemic damage

- **Protect institutions and functions that are central to systemic coherence and development additionality**, rather than applying across-the-board haircuts, when faced with budget cuts (Figure 1.8). Funding decisions should explicitly account for systemic spillovers, i.e. the indirect effects that funding reductions in one part of the system can have on the whole. For example, cuts to leveraged multilateral mechanisms can reduce overall financing volumes by several times the value of the funding reduction because of a reverse leverage effect. Similarly, reductions in funding to central UN entities can disrupt programmes financed by other multilateral development organisations and bilateral donors. Considering these interdependencies can help ensure that short-term fiscal restraint does not produce disproportionate long-term opportunity costs.

- **Strengthen co-ordination among donors to mitigate the risks of correlated and destabilising adjustments.** Increasing transparency over forward funding intentions (such as through DAC surveys and structured discussions at the DAC and with multilateral partners) can provide early warning signals and reduce MDOs' funding uncertainty. Where possible, donors should avoid simultaneous cuts to systemically important institutions whose contraction could trigger cascading effects across low-income and vulnerable contexts.

1.4.2. Recommendations for multilateral development organisations

Adapt structurally to a fragmented and constrained environment

- **Strengthen effectiveness through renewed mandate discipline and a clearer differentiation of comparative advantages**. Institutions need to refocus on areas where they add distinct value, and --where fragmentation undermines impact-- consider rationalising the architecture to reduce overlap and transaction costs. This may involve, where appropriate, organisational mergers or the orderly sunsetting of organisations whose mandates have become redundant or no longer reflect current development priorities, building on approaches such as the portfolio similarity analyses developed by the OECD. In doing so, MDOs should also rethink how structural reforms can help them better respond to the needs and priorities of partner countries. At the same time, as bilateral aid portfolios are increasingly used to pursue donors' geopolitical or national priorities, multilateral channels may need to assume a greater role to protect development objectives that risk being deprioritised, such as poverty reduction or investment in low-income and high fragility contexts.
- **Building resilience through careful diversification and adaptation of MDOs' funding models.** Expanding MDOs' funding base (including through engagement with non-DAC government donors and, where appropriate, private actors) can enhance individual organisations' stability, but must be managed to safeguard governance balance and development additionality. In parts of the system where earmarked contributions have risen steadily in recent years, MDOs' governing bodies may need to review their earmarked portfolios to ensure alignment with their core mandates. They may also consider adapting their budgetary processes, for example by requiring that every earmarked contribution includes a charge-back to core budgets. In parallel, unleveraged organisations, such as most UNDS entities and vertical funds, could investigate opportunities for increasing their catalytic impact through the adoption of innovative financing mechanisms or increased co-financing with MDBs, provided these efforts do not divert them from their institutional mandates.

Treat concessional resources as a strategic asset and not an adjustment variable

- **Safeguard concessional envelopes for the poorest and most vulnerable countries.** This is essential for preserving development additionality and preventing widening financing gaps. Where alternative sources of finance exist, particularly in some middle-income countries, allocation frameworks may need recalibration to protect scarce concessional capacity for sectors where it is indispensable. Protecting sectors with high development impact but limited financial leverage (including humanitarian action, basic services and human capital) is equally critical.
- **Make allocation choices explicit to strengthen accountability and strategic clarity.** Multilateral development organisations should assess, monitor and communicate the allocative impacts of funding reductions, ensuring that distributional consequences across countries, sectors and instruments are understood by their funders and shareholders. In practice, this means tracking how funding cuts affect different country groups and sectors that rely heavily on concessional

resources. Greater transparency on these impacts can inform member states' funding decisions and help ensure that reductions in funding do not inadvertently fall on countries and sectors with limited alternative sources of finance.

- **Sequence grants, blended finance and non-concessional instruments more deliberately so that scarce concessional resources are used where they add the most value**. For example: grants cover what markets will not, blended finance reduce risk, and non-concessional finance can scale investments once conditions allow. This clarity can help avoid situations where scarce concessional resources are used on projects that could have been funded by less subsidised instruments.

References

African Development Bank (2025), *African Development Fund mobilises a historic $11 billion, marking a new era of African ownership and investment-led development*, https://www.afdb.org/en/news-and-events/press-releases/african-development-fund-mobilises-historic-11-billion-marking-new-era-african-ownership-and-investment-led-development-89755. [28]

Bridgetown Initiative (2022), *Bridgetown Initiative on the Reform of the International Development and Climate Finance Architecture*, https://www.bridgetown-initiative.org/. [10]

Dag Hammarskjöld Foundation (2021), *The Way Forward: Fulfilling the Potential of the Funding Compact at the Country Level*, https://www.daghammarskjold.se/wp-content/uploads/2021/11/dhf-funding-compact-2021-web.pdf. [21]

G20 (2024), *Roadmap towards better, bigger and more effective MDBs*, https://coebank.org/documents/1724/G20_Roadmap_towards_better_bigger_and_more_effective_MDBs_T69DXmX.pdf. [9]

G20 Independent Experts Group (2024), *Implementing MDB Reforms: A Stocktake*, Center for Global Development, https://www.cgdev.org/publication/implementing-mdb-reforms-stocktake. [20]

Global Alliance for Vaccines and Immunization (2026), *Overview 2000–2037*, https://www.gavi.org/investing-gavi/funding/overview-2000-2037. [6]

Global Environmental Fund (2022), *Summary of Negotiations of the 8th Replenishment of the GEF Trust Fund*, https://www.thegef.org/council-meeting-documents/gef-c-62-03. [7]

Government of Canada (2026), *Davos 2026: Special address by Mark Carney, Prime Minister of Canada*, https://www.weforum.org/stories/2026/01/davos-2026-special-address-by-mark-carney-prime-minister-of-canada/. [2]

Green Climate Fund (2023), *Report on the outcomes of GCF's second formal replenishment*, https://www.greenclimate.fund/document/gcf-b37-16-rev01. [5]

IDA (2022), *IDA20 - Building Back Better from the Crisis : Toward a Green, Resilient and Inclusive Future*, https://documents.worldbank.org/en/publication/documents-reports/documentdetail/163861645554924417. [3]

IFAD (2025), *2025 Report on IFAD's Development Effectiveness*, https://webapps.ifad.org/members/eb/145/docs/english/EB-2025-145-R-19.pdf?attach=1. [27]

Ihl, J. et al. (2025), "The effectiveness of core and earmarked funding in multilateral development cooperation: Systematic review", *DEval Discussion Paper*, Vol. 02/2025, https://www.deval.org/fileadmin/Redaktion/PDF/05-Publikationen/Berichte/2025_Multilaterale_EZ/DEval-DP-02-2025-MultilateralDC-Web.pdf. [22]

Martinez, N. and J. Estes (2025), *The ABCs of the IFIs: IDA21 Update*, Center for Global Development, https://www.cgdev.org/publication/abcs-ifis. [18]

MOPAN (2025), *Mapping of Multilateral Organisations' Response to the Current Funding Environment*, Multilateral Organisation Performance Assessment Network, Paris, https://www.mopan.org/en/our-work/performance-insights/multilateral-effectiveness-in-a-shifting-landscape/mapping-thematic-brief.html. [26]

OECD (2026), *Creditor Reporting System (dataset)*, https://data-explorer.oecd.org/s/52 (accessed on 15 January 2026). [24]

OECD (2026), *DAC1 table*, http://data-explorer.oecd.org/s/9w (accessed on 22 February 2026). [23]

OECD (2026), *Providers' total use of the multilateral system (database)*, http://data-explorer.oecd.org/s/1td (accessed on 22 February 2026). [16]

OECD (2025), "Cuts in official development assistance: OECD projections for 2025 and the near term", *OECD Policy Briefs*, No. 26, OECD Publishing, Paris, https://doi.org/10.1787/8c530629-en. [17]

OECD (2024), *Multilateral Development Finance 2024*, OECD Publishing, Paris, https://doi.org/10.1787/8f1e2b9b-en. [1]

OECD (2022), *Comparing multilateral and bilateral aid: A portfolio similarity analysis*, OECD Development Perspectives, https://www.oecd.org/en/publications/comparing-multilateral-and-bilateral-aid_81686d2f-en.html. [15]

Rigby, J. (2025), *Global vaccine group Gavi has $9 billion, short of its target*, https://www.reuters.com/business/healthcare-pharmaceuticals/global-vaccine-group-gavi-secures-9-billion-after-funding-summit-2025-06-25/#:~:text=The%20United%20Kingdom%20was%20the,in%20cutting%20international%20aid%20budgets. [19]

Sands, P. (2025), *Transforming Global Health To Maximize Impact And Accelerate Self-Reliance*, https://www.forbes.com/sites/petersands/2025/11/13/transforming-global-health-to-maximize-impact-and-accelerate-self-reliance/. [14]

The Global Fund (2022), *Pledges at Global Fund Seventh Replenishment Conference*, https://archive.theglobalfund.org/media/12328/archive_seventh-replenishment-pledges_list_en.pdf. [4]

U.S. Department of the Treasury (2024), *G7 Finance Ministers and Central Bank Governors' Communiqué*, https://home.treasury.gov/news/press-releases/jy2371. [8]

United Nations (2025), *Resolutions adopted by the General Assembly on 30 December 2025*, https://docs.un.org/en/A/RES/80/244%20A-C. [13]

United Nations (2025), "United Nations revises 2026 regular budget proposal, pairing cost reductions with initial reform measures", *UN News*, https://news.un.org/en/story/2025/09/1165850. [11]

United Nations (2024), *Resolutions adopted by the General Assembly on 24 December 2024*, https://digitallibrary.un.org/record/4071044?ln=en&v=pdf. [12]

WFP (2025), *Food Security Impact of Reduction in WFP Funding*, https://docs.wfp.org/api/documents/WFP-0000166581/download/. [25]

World Bank Group (2023), *IDA20 Mid-term Review*, World Bank Group, Washington DC, https://thedocs.worldbank.org/en/doc/f1d0b477064fadf03bd4e4aa96b5b63d-0410012023/original/ida-20-MTR-factsheet-11-16-2020.pdf. [29]

2 The landscape of multilateral development co-operation

This chapter examines the evolving landscape of multilateral development co-operation, mapping the institutions and financing modalities that shape the multilateral development system. It shows how its historically expanding and increasingly diverse architecture is coming under growing strain from geopolitical fragmentation, declining trust in multilateral approaches and pressures on aid budgets. The chapter reaffirms the critical role of multilateral development co-operation in sustaining collective development outcomes in a more contested and constrained global environment. At the same time, it argues that the system needs a reset – to adapt its institutional configuration and operating practices to the demands of the global development agenda and to safeguard multilateral coherence, development impact and effectiveness.

2.1. Understanding the multilateral development system and its financial structure

2.1.1. *The system's architecture is multifaceted and interconnected*

Today's multilateral development system is made up of more than 200 organisations. Known as multilateral development organisations (MDOs), they are defined in this report as those institutions with a sustainable development or humanitarian mandate and a governance structure based on multiple sovereign members. They include the entities that are part of the United Nations Development System (UNDS), multilateral development banks (MDBs), an expanding set of issue-specific financing facilities (vertical funds) and other institutions with specific institutional arrangements. Figure 2.1 shows the central role played by the multilateral development system as a channel of development co-operation.

Figure 2.1. The multilateral development system serves as a major conduit for development co-operation

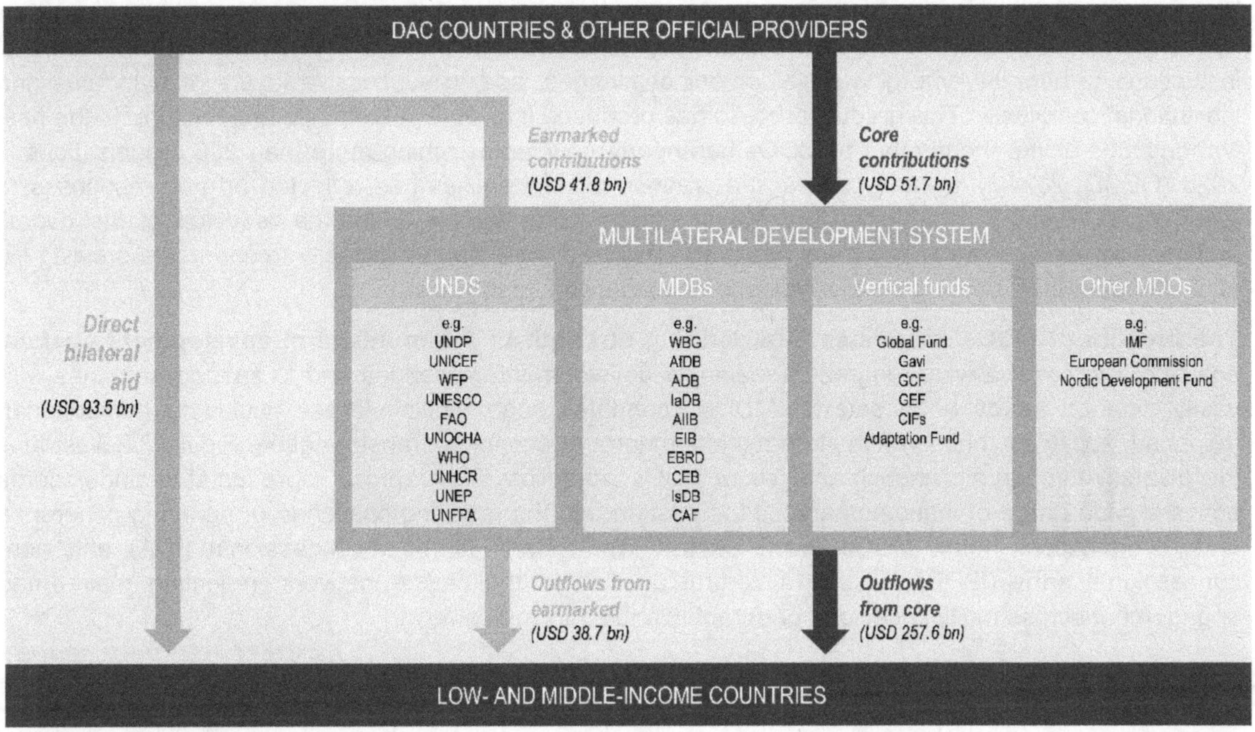

Note: The table presents a non-exhaustive list of multilateral development organisations. Their acronyms are explained in the list at the front of the report.
Source: Authors' design based on (OECD, 2026[1]), "OECD DAC Annex 2 - List of ODA-eligible international organisations", available at https://webfs.oecd.org/oda/DataCollection/Resources/OECD-ODA-Single-Table-2026-for-2025-flows.xlsx.

Two main official funding modalities – core and earmarked – underpin the functioning of the multilateral development system, with the balance between them having major implications for how the system operates. Core contributions refer to flexible resources provided by donors to MDOs. The MDOs can choose, within an overarching strategy, how they should be used to deliver on their mandates, invest in institutional capacities and respond to evolving needs. In the UNDS system, core resources take two main forms: "assessed contributions", which are mandatory and calculated based on donors' income, and "voluntary core contributions", provided at donors' discretion. In MDBs, core support is primarily provided through capital subscriptions from shareholders, as well as through voluntary contributions to concessional windows replenished periodically. Similarly, many vertical funds rely on periodic replenishment cycles through which donors provide resources to support their mandates. Non-core contributions, also known as earmarked or multi-bi aid, are bilateral resources channelled through MDOs but earmarked by donors for specific countries, themes or programmes, often through trust funds. This earmarking allows member states to retain a degree of control over their use. As examined further in Chapter 3, while earmarking can help target emerging priorities, it has also been shown to fragment funding, increase transaction costs and reduce multilateral flexibility (Ihl et al., 2025[2]) (Graham, 2017[3]). The balance between core and earmarked contributions not only affects individual organisations – it also shapes the coherence of the multilateral development system as a whole.

MDOs vary significantly in their core functions (financing, implementation, standard-setting) as well as in their thematic and geographic mandates (from universal to niche). Another key differentiating factor is the mix of instruments they deploy, ranging from grants and loans to guarantees, equity and technical co-operation. This instrument mix strongly influences the scale of financing each MDO can provide. Governance models and membership structures also diverge, including differences in the voice afforded to low- and middle-income countries in decision making.

The system we know today is the result of a steady and cumulative expansion since its inception in the aftermath of the Second World War. Over decades, countries have established new multilateral institutions to address emerging development challenges, adding successive layers of mandates and institutional complexity. This gradual process has produced a diverse yet intricate architecture. In the past two decades alone, the number of MDOs has nearly doubled, reaching more than 200 organisations in 2020 (OECD, 2024[4]). In many cases, the creation of new entities has reflected ad hoc responses to emerging challenges and shifting political priorities, rather than a deliberate redesign of the overall architecture. As a result, this process has both increased the system's capacity to address a growing list of challenges while contributing to a more complex network of institutions.

The breadth of MDOs' mandates is a defining strength of the multilateral development system, enabling it to cover a wide range of sustainable development challenges and to support countries with vastly different needs and contexts. MDOs' mandates span multiple areas, including humanitarian response, social sectors, infrastructure development and economic transformation. Figure 2.2 illustrates this diversity through a clustering analysis of MDOs' portfolios: this graphical representation underscores both the wide range of mandates across the system and the resulting challenge of ensuring coherence and co-ordination. Some MDOs, such as the World Bank Group's concessional (IDA) and non-concessional arms (IBRD), occupy a central position in the cluster network, reflecting their broad engagement across multiple sectors, geographic and financing contexts.

Figure 2.2. The system involves myriad organisations addressing a wide range of sustainable development issues

Clustering (t-SNE) of multilateral development organisations by dominant aid portfolio, 2015-2023 average

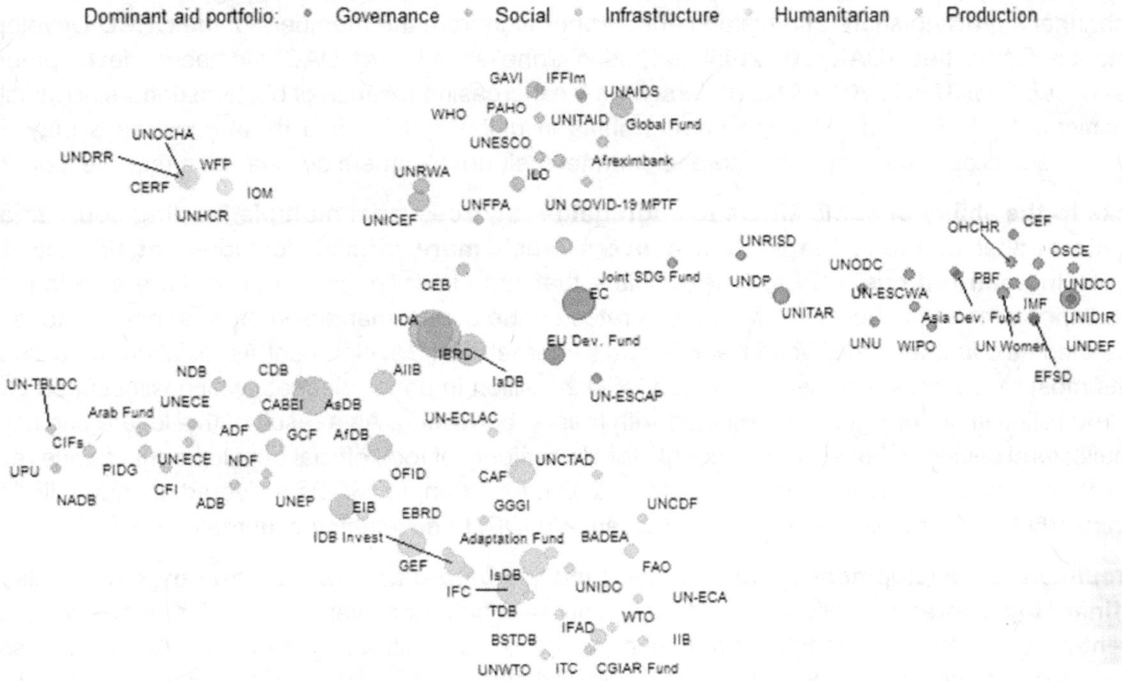

Note: t-distributed stochastic neighbour embedding (t-SNE) clusters are based on the five following macro-sectors: governance, social, infrastructure, humanitarian and production. The colour legend distinguishes between the dominant aid portfolio for each multilateral development organisation. Organisations positioned closer together in the map have more similar aid portfolios, while those further apart have more distinct sectoral profiles. The size of bubbles reflects MDOs' outflows.
Source: Authors' calculations based on OECD (2026[5]), *Creditor Reporting System* (dataset), https://data-explorer.oecd.org/s/52.

Beyond MDOs and their member states, the system relies on a broader network of stakeholders that channel, co-finance, implement and benefit from multilateral development co-operation activities. Member states remain the primary funders of most MDOs, but private actors (including philanthropies) are becoming increasingly important in some parts of the system, especially for vertical funds and some UNDS entities. For some MDOs, other multilateral organisations, civil society organisations and private investors sometimes act as implementing partners or co-financiers.

Low and middle-income countries, while being the main beneficiaries of these activities, are also shareholders and, in some cases, contributors to the financing of certain MDOs. Their triple role as recipients, shareholders and donors underscores the importance of governance arrangements, voice and accountability within the system. This is especially true in a context where traditional donors face growing constraints in maintaining their contribution levels, and where multilateral organisations may need to look more actively at a wider range of contributors and financing sources to help fill funding gaps. This is exemplified by the recent replenishment of the African Development Fund (ADF, the African Development Bank's concessional window): despite the absence of some traditional donors, the ADF reached a record-high replenishment thanks in part to new and emerging donors stepping up to fill the gap. Notably, the number of pledging African countries more than tripled compared to the previous ADF replenishment, with 19 African countries making their first ever contributions to the fund (African Development Fund, 2025[6]). Such developments point to an evolution in the participation of developing countries in the financing and governance of multilateral development institutions.

2.1.2. *Multilateral development co-operation covers a wide spectrum of needs, risks and financing contexts*

MDOs are a core pillar of the development co-operation architecture and key delivery partners for bilateral development co-operation. Previous editions of this report have highlighted that MDOs receive and channel a growing share of development co-operation from the members of the OECD Development Assistance Committee (DAC). In 2024, MDOs channelled 41% of DAC members' development co-operation, up from 37% in 2010. This underscores the increasing reliance of bilateral donors on multilateral mechanisms to deliver aid, although current shifts in global politics and fiscal constraints may prompt donors to reconsider how they prioritise and channel their development co-operation (see Section 2.2).

Thanks to the ability of some MDOs to aggregate resources from multiple funding sources and to leverage capital markets, the system delivers much more official development finance than it receives in contributions. MDBs, for example – thanks to their financing model – are able to leverage their balance sheets and borrow at favourable rates on the capital markets in order to on-lend to low- and middle-income countries. The World Bank Group's International Development Association (IDA) illustrates this: its most recent replenishment mobilised USD 24 billion in donor pledges, which will support close to USD 100 billion in financing once combined with market borrowing. As a result of this leveraging capacity, the multilateral development system accounts for the majority of total official development finance received by developing countries over the past decade. In 2024, for example, MDOs delivered or channelled nearly two-thirds (60%) of total official development finance (ODF) to developing countries.

The multilateral development system is designed to operate across a broad range of needs, risks and financing contexts. Collectively, MDOs support countries at various development stages and in different areas, with roles ranging from responding to humanitarian needs and delivering essential services, to financing large-scale public investment and mobilising private capital (Figure 2.3). This breadth is a core strength of the system, as it allows different organisations to fulfil distinct roles while contributing to shared development objectives. Understanding how these roles relate to one another is essential for assessing whether the system's architecture remains coherent and fit for purpose, particularly in a context of rising demands and tighter resources. Figure 2.3 illustrates these relationships, while recognising that in practice they may overlap and interact in more complex ways.

Figure 2.3. Multilateral organisations are designed to play complementary roles, providing development finance across different contexts

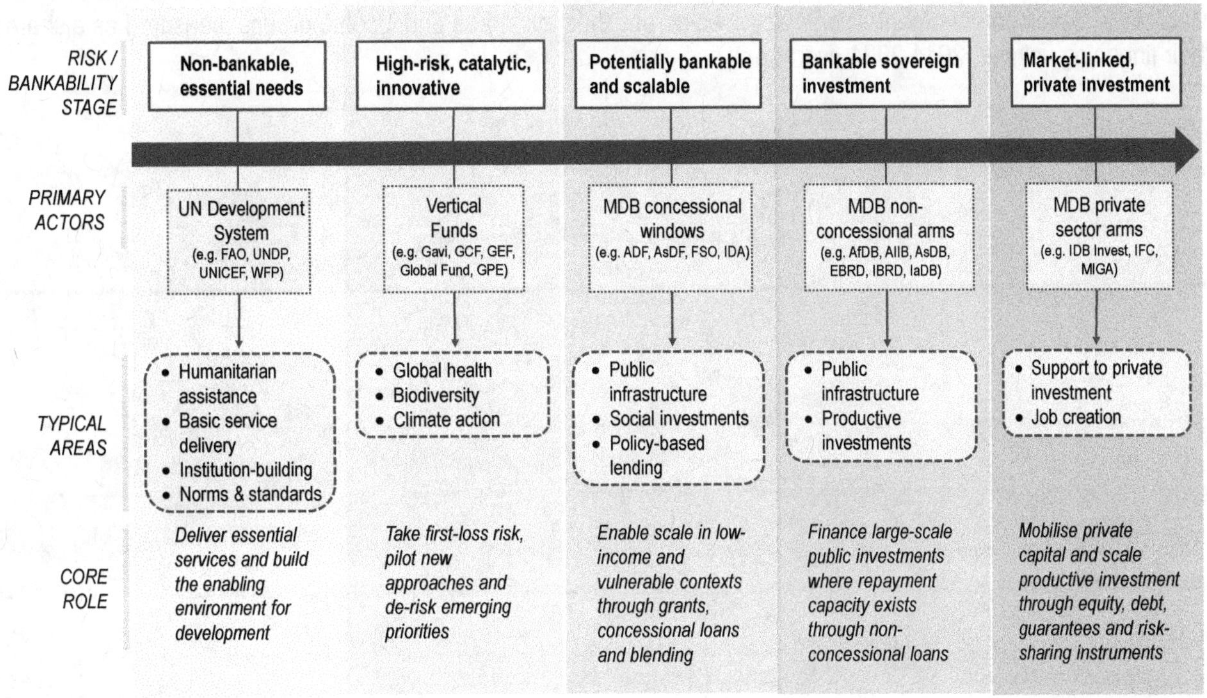

At the non-bankable end of the spectrum, the UNDS plays a foundational role by building the ecosystem that underpins development and delivering essential services. The matrix in Figure 2.4 confirms this role, showing a strong concentration of UNDS activity in humanitarian assistance and to a lesser extent in social sectors. These activities are rarely bankable and often take place in highly fragile or crisis-affected contexts but they are indispensable for protecting lives, maintaining basic service provision and building institutional capacity. Beyond immediate delivery, UNDS investments also help create the enabling environment (e.g. through governance, norms, data and human capital) without which neither public nor private finance can operate effectively.

Vertical funds typically occupy the catalytic segment of the spectrum to support global public goods and collective action. Their strong investment in global public goods, such as health, education, climate and biodiversity, reflects their mandate to address specific issues where markets fail and collective action is required. The matrix shows that some vertical funds also have a significant footprint in infrastructure-related areas, largely related to green investments. They often play a de-risking role, piloting new approaches, absorbing early-stage risk and demonstrating viability, with the expectation that successful approaches can be scaled through concessional or non-concessional MDB financing, often in collaboration with UNDS entities and other partners for implementation at country level.

Figure 2.4. Multilateral roles connect along a broadly logical progression from higher risk needs to more bankable forms of finance

Multilateral development organisations' activities across thematic areas and income groups measured as a share of their financing volume, 2014-2024 average

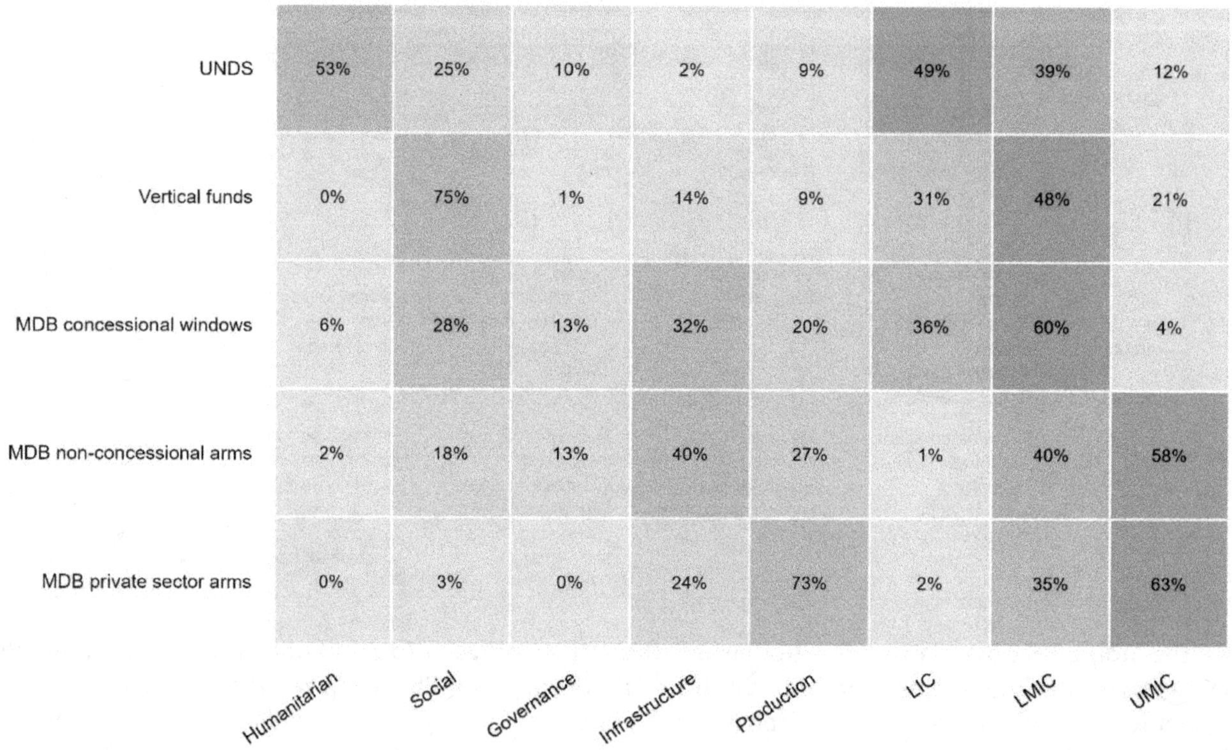

Note: The chart should be interpreted by organisation row, whereby darker green indicates higher activity within a thematic area and darker red depicts higher activity within a country income group. Colours are not comparable across rows. LIC=low-income country; LMIC=lower-middle income country; UMIC=upper-middle income country.
Source: Authors' calculations based on OECD (2026[5]), *Creditor Reporting System* (dataset), https://data-explorer.oecd.org/s/52.

MDB concessional windows sit at the centre of the spectrum, transforming high-risk investments into scalable opportunities. The matrix shows these windows to be strongly engaged in both social and infrastructure sectors, reflecting their dual mandate: supporting essential public investments while enabling large-scale financing (Figure 2.4). By blending grants and highly concessional loans, MDB concessional windows reduce risk to levels that allow projects to proceed in low-income and vulnerable contexts.

At the more bankable end of the spectrum, MDB non-concessional arms and private sector arms focus on scaling infrastructure and productive investment. The matrix shows a strong concentration of non-concessional MDB financing in infrastructure, and of private sector arms in production-related activities, consistent with their mandates to mobilise capital, crowd in private finance and achieve scale (Figure 2.4). These institutions play a critical role in providing financing for larger-scale investment in contexts that no longer require heavy de-risking efforts. However, their effectiveness depends on the functioning of the upstream parts of the financing chain, including catalytic public sector lending that helps strengthen the enabling environment for market-based finance.

Maintaining a clear and coherent division of labour across the multilateral development system requires proactive attention from MDOs' member states and governing bodies. In a context of heightened pressure on development resources, organisations may face incentives either to expand into new areas to pursue funding opportunities or, conversely, to refocus on core mandates. While such adaptation can be justified in specific circumstances or at the institutional level, it can also end up blurring the logical division of roles across the system as a whole. In this sense, the financing spectrum presented above, while simplified and non-exhaustive, can serve as a broad compass for system stewardship: by situating multilateral activities along different risk and financing contexts, it helps clarify where each type of institution (i.e. grant-based versus leveraged) adds the most value. At the same time, financing modalities are only one dimension of comparative advantage; other factors, including institutional mandates, operational capabilities and system-wide functions, also shape the appropriate division of labour across organisations (MOPAN, 2026[7]).

The large footprint and ability of MDOs to operate across all contexts positions them as key actors of the post-Sevilla Financing for Development landscape. Recent international discussions on financing for development have re-emphasised country ownership and country-led development as central principles for delivering impactful support to developing countries in an increasingly constrained financing environment (United Nations, 2025[8]). The differentiated roles of multilateral development organisations across the risk and bankability spectrum provide an important mechanism for sequencing financing modalities in ways that reflect country priorities and capacities, and thus align external resources with national development strategies.

Multilateral development organisations are also well placed to support this agenda because they have country ownership embedded in their institutional and operational models. Evidence from the 2023-26 Monitoring Round of the Global Partnership for Effective Development Co-operation (GPEDC) shows that many UNDS organisations rely on extensive stakeholder consultation to design programmes, including of vulnerable and marginalised groups of the population (OECD/UNDP, forthcoming[9]). MDBs, meanwhile, work largely through countries' public finance management systems, aligning their lending operations with national development plans and budgetary frameworks. GPEDC data confirm this comparative advantage further: on average, MDOs tend to outperform their bilateral peers on key effectiveness measurements, including on indicators related to country ownership (Figure 2.5). These findings suggest that the value of the multilateral development system lies not only in the scale of resources it mobilises, but also in how it delivers them.

Figure 2.5. Multilateral organisations tend to outperform bilateral actors on key measures of development co-operation effectiveness

Scores from selected development co-operation effectiveness indicators, bilateral vs multilateral average

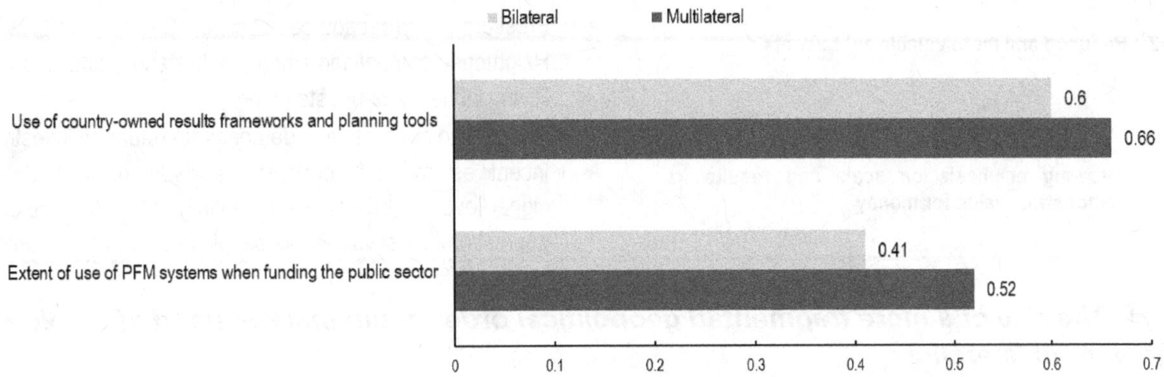

Source: OECD/UNDP (forthcoming[9]), *Making Development Co-operation More Effective - 2026 Progress Report.*

While the breadth of multilateral roles and the characteristics of MDOs' operational models allow the system to deliver collective value that is greater than the sum of individual donor efforts, this collective value should not be taken for granted. It depends critically on factors such as sustained trust in collective action and shared institutions, as well as stable and predictable funding. These foundations are now being tested by a convergence of geopolitical and fiscal pressures that are reshaping incentives, weakening funding models and raising fundamental questions about the system's capacity to adapt without undermining its core functions. The multilateral development architecture now operates in a context of heightened contestation over its role, legitimacy and effectiveness, with several large donors reducing their development co-operation budgets. These dynamics, explored in greater depth in the next section, raise questions not only about the volume of multilateral development finance, but also about the type of institutional configuration that is emerging in the system, the configuration that may be required to address future development challenges, and the configuration that can be sustained in a more constrained financing environment.

2.2. Pressure on multiple fronts means the multilateral development system must adapt to survive

The multilateral development system is facing growing pressures to adapt in a rapidly changing development co-operation landscape. While long-standing concerns about the complexity of the multilateral development architecture, and the quantity and quality of donor contributions, have shaped debates on the effectiveness of multilateral development co-operation, the current context introduces a more acute set of risks. The following sections examine three pressures reshaping incentives and funding models: geopolitical fragmentation and declining trust, tighter and more volatile aid budgets, and growing scrutiny of value for money (Table 2.1).

Table 2.1. Intensifying pressures are pushing the multilateral development system to adapt

Pressures and drivers of adaptation	How they undermine the multilateral development system
1. **Geopolitical fragmentation and declining trust**	• Erosion of consensus-based funding and governance • Shift in global aid towards domestic and strategic interests • Incentives to use more discretionary (i.e. earmarked) funding
2. **Reduced and more volatile aid budgets**	• Weakened predictability of funding • Pressure on core resources • Heightened competition among multilateral institutions • Rising influence of private actors
3. **Growing emphasis on scale and results to demonstrate value for money**	• Pressure to cut costs and demonstrate return on investment • Incentives to shift portfolios towards easier-to-deliver, higher-leverage operations, potentially at the expense of the poorest and most vulnerable people in high-fragility contexts

2.2.1. *The rise of a more fragmented geopolitical order could mark the end of a golden age of multilateralism*

Geopolitical tensions are reshaping incentives within the multilateral development system and accelerating a shift away from collective approaches. As donors' trust in the international rules-based order and multilateral system weakens, decisions about multilateral funding and engagement are increasingly driven by national priorities rather than assessments of global needs and systemic efficiency. For example, the United States recently announced its withdrawal from several international organisations and initiatives, citing concerns that their mandates were inconsistent with US national interest (Government of the United States, 2026[10]). Given the United States' historical role as a central supporter of the multilateral system, such decisions carry significant implications for the stability and predictability of multilateral engagement. In addition, they may incentivise MDOs to accommodate donor preferences in order to secure resources, even when this comes at the expense of strategic coherence.

The multilateral development system was initially designed to function as a collective investment. Thanks to relatively predictable, flexible contributions, the system was able to pool resources, leverage contributions and benefit from economies of scale, as already discussed in Section 2.1. This co-operative environment underpinned the system's capacity to support a large and growing set of programmes in low- and middle-income countries and to finance global public goods. This is illustrated by the green quadrant in Figure 2.6.

In contrast, the current context increasingly resembles a prisoner's dilemma, in which both donors and MDOs face incentives to act in ways that are individually rational but collectively sub-optimal. Over time, however, donors have progressively favoured more discretionary and earmarked forms of engagement to maximise control and visibility over their contributions, while MDOs faced incentives to expand their mandates and resources. This trend has accelerated in recent years, with some donors withdrawing their support to the multilateral development system (orange quadrants, Figure 2.6). At the same time, some multilateral organisations may respond to pressures by seeking to secure resources through mission creep and greater reliance on earmarked funding.

These strategies may help individual actors secure short-term gains, but they also reinforce fragmentation, increase transaction costs and weaken system-wide coherence. As illustrated by the red quadrant in Figure 2.6, declining trust and non-co-operative adjustments on both sides can ultimately push the system towards a low-co-operation equilibrium in which leverage declines, multilateral financing becomes more fragmented and overall delivery capacity weakens. Exiting this low-co-operation equilibrium carries significant political and financial costs, underscoring the importance of preventing the system from reaching this tipping point in the first place.

Figure 2.6. Donors' incentives increasingly resemble a prisoner's dilemma

	Other donors cooperate	Other donors defect
Donor A cooperates	**Payoff: High** • Burden-sharing. • Multilateral core funding remains predictable. • MDOs can plan and deliver at scale, preserving collective effectiveness. • Spillovers reduce fragility and crisis spill-back to both donor and partner countries.	**Payoff: Medium** • Donor A shoulders more of the multilateral burden amid others' cuts, creating risk of moral hazard/"free riders". • Multilateral effectiveness erodes as MDOs scale back and triage. • However, reputational benefits and strategic influence inside multilaterals persist.
Donor A defects	**Payoff: Medium** • Donor A benefits from fiscal savings and ability to prioritise domestic/bilateral goals. • Donor A free-rides on others' multilateral spending. • Systemic risk rises, and donor A forfeits influence, burden-sharing, and pooled crisis tools.	**Payoff: Low** • Widespread cuts lead to steep collective underfunding, fragmentation, and weaker global public goods (health security, humanitarian response). • MDOs downsize and crisis response falters • Long-run costs (conflict, migration crises, pandemics) increase for all.

Low-co-operation equilibrium

This growing geopolitical fragmentation is also encouraging a shift from broad-based multilateral co-operation towards "minilateralism", whereby small coalitions collaborate on more narrowly defined issues. With broad-based consensus harder to sustain and trust in collective arrangements eroding, both donors and institutions increasingly seek alternative ways to advance priorities without relying on quasi-universal agreement. One visible response to this environment is a growing reliance on coalition-based forms of multilateral engagement. For example, previous editions of this report have highlighted the growing number of vertical funds and other specific-purpose funding mechanisms observed since the early 2000s (OECD, 2024[4]) (OECD, 2020[11]). While part of this evolution reflects a search for specialisation as core development themes are already covered by long-established institutions and new initiatives seek to demonstrate relevance by focusing on gaps or emerging priorities, it is also shaped by the growing difficulty of sustaining broad-based commitments. Figure 2.7 illustrates how this shift has progressively transformed the multilateral architecture and contributed to the proliferation of multilateral development organisations. In this sense, the "variable geometry" multilateralism invoked by some political leaders (Government of Canada, 2026[12]) reflects in part the intensification of a longer-term trend, now accelerated by growing contestation of multilateralism and increasingly divergent priorities among donors.

In contexts and areas where consensus is difficult to achieve, coalition-based approaches can help drive progress on specific global challenges where credible implementation capacity is ensured, but they carry risks. In the case of vertical funds, the implementation capacity is often ensured by relying on established multilateral organisations with country presence, such as UNDS entities and MDBs. While this approach can be more efficient than creating parallel delivery structures, it also carries risk, including an additional co-ordination burden for traditional MDOs, which themselves are under strain from sharp donor cuts. More broadly, the continued multiplication of issue-specific initiatives raises concerns over further fragmentation and institutional proliferation within the multilateral development architecture, potentially weakening system-wide coherence over time.

Figure 2.7. The multilateral development architecture is evolving from broad-based donorship to narrower issue-specific coalitions

Multilateral development organisations by date of establishment and number of government donors in 2024

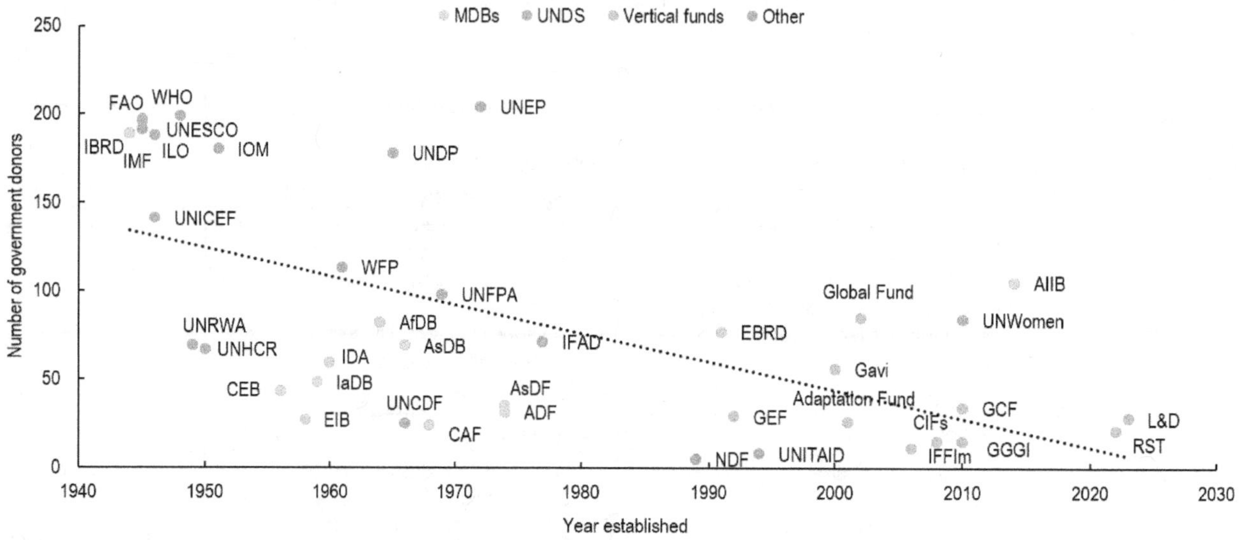

Note: Although UN Women may appear to be an outlier of the UNDS on this graph, it should be noted that the creation of UN Women in 2010 resulted from the merger of four pre-existing entities: the UN Division of the Advancement of Women (DAW), the UN International Research and Training Institute for the Advancement of Women (INSTRAW), the UN Office of the Special Advisor on Gender Issues (OSAGI), and the UN Development Fund for Women (UNIFEM).

Source: Authors' calculations based on OECD (2026[5]), *Providers' Total Use of the Multilateral System* (dataset), http://data-explorer.oecd.org/s/1td.

A similar dynamic is visible in multilateral fora, where informal coalitions have gained prominence, sometimes in place of formal multilateral processes. Recently, some international negotiations have accommodated coalition-based approaches as a pragmatic response to diverging interests, enabling groups of like-minded actors to move forward on what they perceive as priorities without being constrained by the need for broad-based agreement. This logic was evident at the Fourth International Conference on Financing for Development's (FfD4) Sevilla Platform for Action (SPA), with the platform attracting 130 voluntary initiatives by various coalitions of actors at its launch in 2025 (United Nations, 2025[13]). The SPA and similar approaches signal an acceptance that progress on certain issues – such as innovative financing mechanisms, technical assistance, or thematic priorities supported by subsets of countries – may need to proceed through relatively small and informal coalitions rather than seek broad-based consensus.

However, while such coalitions can generate momentum when broad-based consensus is difficult to achieve, they also risk creating a "collective action vacuum" if they displace formal multilateral processes without having the capacity required for delivery. Unlike multilateral institutions, informal coalitions often lack durable governance structures, predictable funding and accountability mechanisms. When political commitments are made through such coalitions without being anchored in institutions responsible for their implementation, co-ordination, monitoring and reporting may remain superficial or, at best, uneven. In these cases, coalitions can create the appearance of collective action while weakening the institutional infrastructure needed to translate commitments into action, further straining an already fragmented multilateral development system. On the other hand, when established multilateral development organisations are tasked with supporting or monitoring these coalition-based initiatives, resources and attention can be diverted from system-wide priorities toward narrower agendas, particularly if the required support is not explicitly acknowledged or properly funded.

The geopolitical tensions described in this section are coinciding with tightening fiscal constraints in donor countries, amplifying the risks facing the multilateral development system. While geopolitical fragmentation and declining trust in collective action weaken the political foundations of multilateralism, the emerging aid crisis, in part linked to financial issues faced by donor countries, directly threatens the funding flows that sustain multilateral institutions. Reduced fiscal space, shifting domestic priorities and growing scrutiny of international spending are translating into aid budget cuts among several major contributors to the multilateral development system. The next section examines how these fiscal pressures are already starting to affect the system.

2.2.2. *The global aid crisis threatens to unravel the financial foundations of multilateral development co-operation*

The development co-operation landscape is entering a period of acute financial stress, often referred to as a global crisis of aid. In 2025, 11 DAC members officially announced substantial reductions to their aid budgets, signalling a break with the expansionary trend that characterised the multilateral development system in previous decades (OECD, 2025[14]). These 11 DAC members, which include several of the largest contributors to the system, such as the United States, United Kingdom, Germany and France, collectively accounted for 63% of DAC members' multilateral funding in 2024 (Figure 2.8).

Figure 2.8. The 11 DAC members cutting their ODA in 2025-27 accounted for roughly two-thirds of total DAC contributions to the system in 2024

Share of DAC members' multilateral contributions, 2024

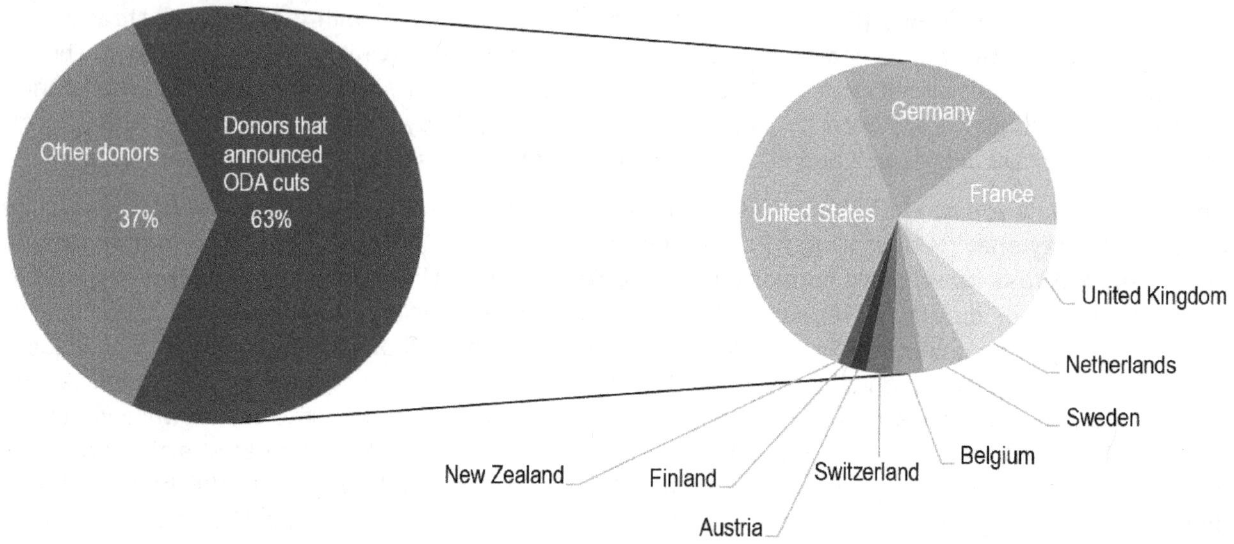

Note: Calculations are based on disbursements, in 2024 constant prices.
Source: Authors' calculations based on OECD (2026[15]), *Providers' Total Use of the Multilateral System* (dataset), http://data-explorer.oecd.org/s/1td.

This aid crisis reflects the convergence of several reinforcing pressures that are simultaneously constraining political, fiscal and institutional support for development co-operation. Political backing for international development has weakened in parts of the donor community, while rising uncertainty about the geopolitical and economic outlook is also shaping how governments approach development co-operation. At the same time, fiscal constraints driven by the recent series of global shocks (e.g. COVID-19, Russia's war of aggression against Ukraine) and the prioritisation of military spending, are narrowing fiscal space. These pressures are compounded by the severe liquidity shortages across the UN, which hosts many multilateral development organisations.

While bilateral aid agencies appeared to bear the brunt of the aid cuts initially, the multilateral development system is far from insulated from these shocks. Reductions in bilateral aid budgets, the downsizing or dismantling of development co-operation agencies, and the merging of aid portfolios into ministries of foreign affairs have made the headlines. Yet, strains are also emerging across multilateral development organisations, including increased funding volatility and uncertainty, as well as organisational adjustments such as staffing reductions and programme down-scaling. The projections presented in Chapter 3 suggest that this reduction in funding to the multilateral development system is likely to be sustained in the coming years. However, the exact extent to which these pressures translate into reduced multilateral funding will depend on how donors allocate cuts between bilateral and multilateral channels: reductions may be transmitted symmetrically across both, fall disproportionately on multilateral contributions, or be partly offset if donors shift a larger share of constrained budgets through multilateral mechanisms.

Recent withdrawals and defunding decisions by major donors underscore the vulnerability of multilateral organisations to domestic political cycles and fiscal pressures. Decisions such as the withdrawal of the United States from several UN entities and funding windows illustrate how rapidly national political shifts can translate into abrupt financing shocks for multilateral institutions. As described in

Section 3.1.2, these episodes highlight a structural fragility of the system: many MDOs depend heavily on a small number of dominant contributors, making them particularly exposed to policy reversals in a handful of member states.

More fundamentally, there is a growing risk that aid budget cuts will have asymmetrical and amplified effects through multilateral development finance. Historically, one of the multilateral development system's key comparative advantages has been its ability to leverage member contributions by pooling and leveraging resources to mobilise financing at scale. As highlighted in the last edition of this report, each dollar channelled by DAC members to the multilateral development system generates, on average, three dollars in sustainable development finance, reflecting the strong leverage power of the system (OECD, 2024[4]).

The danger today is that cuts could see the leverage turn negative, whereby even relatively modest cuts in member contributions lead to disproportionately large reductions in multilateral output (see also Section 4.2.1). As multilateral contributions decline, leverage mechanisms weaken, co-financing falls and institutional capacity contracts, magnifying the impact of initial budget reductions. The scale of this effect will depend critically on where cuts occur, as some multilateral organisations and funding modalities preserve multilateral leverage better than others. In this context, uncoordinated funding decisions taken by individual donors risk producing system-wide consequences that extend far beyond their immediate fiscal savings.

Faced with the combined pressures of geopolitical fragmentation and tightening fiscal constraints in major donor countries, the multilateral development system is entering a phase in which adaptation is unavoidable. These conditions are accelerating the reform momentum across the system, not only as a response to immediate financial stress but also as an attempt to preserve relevance, legitimacy and delivery capacity in a more constrained environment. The next section examines how ongoing reform initiatives are reshaping the multilateral development system, and whether they are equipping it to adapt to these pressures or merely enabling short-term survival.

2.2.3. Cost efficiency considerations are driving multilateral reform

Political and financial imperatives are driving multilateral reform in ways that risk sidelining effectiveness goals. In a context of tightening budgets and heightened scrutiny from multilateral stakeholders, reform agendas are often framed around demonstrating value for money, maximising leverage and containing costs, rather than addressing long-standing structural challenges. While these reforms respond to real and pressing constraints, the risk is that short-term financial and political imperatives could crowd out deeper efforts to strengthen effectiveness, accountability and collective outcomes.

This tension is visible in the current wave of MDB reform, where the focus has shifted in response to evolving shareholder priorities and tighter fiscal space in major donor countries. Early reform narratives, such as the Bridgetown Initiative, emphasised expanding MDB mandates to scale up financing for global public goods, with climate action occupying a central place alongside traditional development objectives (Bridgetown Initiative, 2022[16]). More recently, MDB reform discussions have increasingly centred on balance sheet optimisation, capital adequacy adjustments and financial innovation, alongside a renewed emphasis on economic growth and job creation. The World Bank leadership, for example, has placed job creation at the heart of its strategy for the coming years (Banga, 2025[17]). This reorientation of the MDB reform drive reflects in part an effort to adapt to domestic political shifts in major shareholders like the United States, although it also aligns with the strong emphasis that many low- and middle-income countries place on economic growth and employment.

A concrete illustration of the MDB reform reorientation towards capital efficiency is the launch of the World Bank Group's new Guarantee Platform in 2024 as part of the institution's broader

evolution agenda. Housed in the Multilateral Investment Guarantee Agency (MIGA) and bringing together guarantee expertise from the World Bank, IFC and MIGA under a single structure, the platform aims to streamline products and enable the institution to operate increasingly as a "leveraging bank" rather than primarily a lending bank (World Bank Group, 2025[18]). Guarantees are attractive in a constrained fiscal environment because they can mobilise multiples of private capital relative to the capital they consume. However, the difference they make to development depends on careful targeting. In this sense, the Guarantee Platform embodies both the promise and the tension at the heart of current MDB reform: the pursuit of scale and leverage must remain aligned with country needs and the system's broader collective mandate.

Recent MDB reforms have increased leverage, but donor investment in these institutions has not kept pace with increasingly ambitious lending targets. With many MDBs continuing to operate under zero-growth administrative budgeting, bottlenecks to MDB ambition are likely to be institutional, reflecting underinvestment in staff, technical skills and systems. Signs of these pressures are already evident in several multilateral development banks, underscoring the need for a more holistic approach to strengthening MDB capacity. For example, from 2008 to 2024, the combined IBRD-IDA portfolio volume grew by 127% in real terms, while administrative expenditure contracted by 2% over the same horizon (World Bank, 2024[19]). In its FY2025 budget document, the World Bank highlighted the need for greater investment in staff resources and skills to maintain this growth trajectory (World Bank, 2024[19]).

Within the United Nations system, reform pressures are being driven by acute financial stress, with liquidity constraints shaping both the pace and substance of change. Persistent and substantial arrears, and growing criticism from major member state donors, have pushed the UN system into a position where short-term financial survival has become a central concern. In this context, the reduction of the UN 2026 programme budget by USD 270 million compared to 2025 (Figure 2.9), and the UN Secretary General's proposal to reduce the institution's workforce by 19% (United Nations, 2025[20]), underscore the extent to which reform is being driven by constraints. While these measures may be unavoidable in the face of immediate liquidity challenges, caution is required to ensure they do not end up crowding out longer-term reforms aimed at improving coherence, mandate clarity and system-wide impact, particularly at a time when demands on the UNDS, and in particular its humanitarian entities, continue to expand.

Figure 2.9. The UN's programme budget and staff cuts reflect efforts to enhance cost efficiency

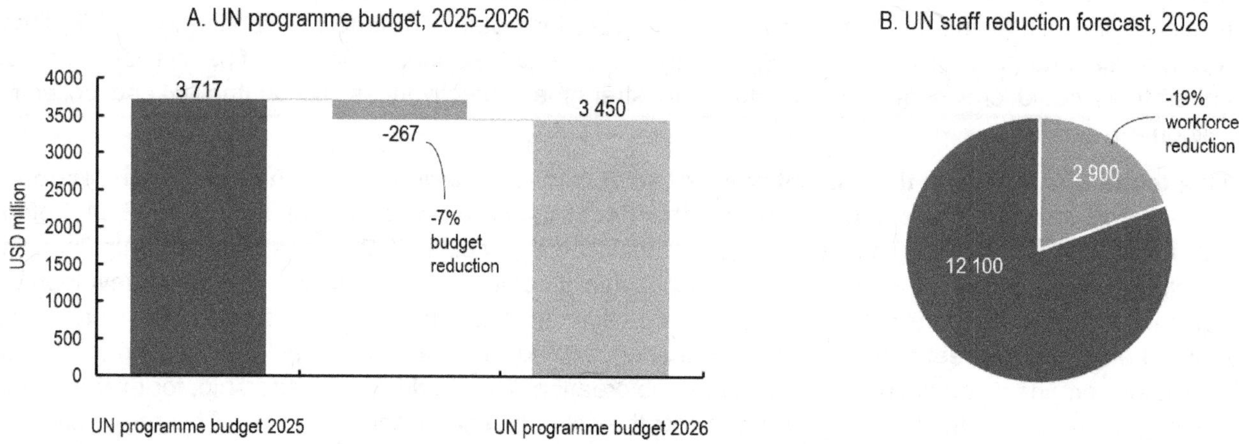

Note: The UN programme budget is used primarily to finance the operating, staff, and programme expenses of the UN's main organs (General Assembly, Security Council, Economic and Social Council, Secretariat and International Court of Justice).
Source: Authors' calculations based on United Nations (2024[21]), *Resolutions Adopted by the General Assembly on 24 December 2024*, https://digitallibrary.un.org/record/4071044?ln=en&v=pdf; and United Nations (2025[22]), *Resolutions Adopted by the General Assembly on 30 December 2025*, https://docs.un.org/en/A/RES/80/244%20A-C.

Despite being driven largely by political and financial imperatives, the current wave of reform creates openings to address some long-standing structural weaknesses of the system. For many years, concerns have been raised about institutional proliferation, overlapping mandates and limited system-wide transparency on results and impact. The severity of current financial pressures may increase the political space to revisit these issues more seriously than in the past, including by exploring options for rationalising functions where mandates have become redundant or where a single entity could deliver on the agenda of several. Figure 2.10, Panel A shows that some sectors tend to have a greater incidence of overlapping multilateral aid portfolios, even within the same country, contributing to a crowded operating environment for MDOs. Of all the sectors, health exhibits the highest degree of overlap in MDOs' country-sector portfolios. While such overlap can reflect intentional co-ordination, it also underscores the importance of clear role differentiation and strong co-ordination mechanisms to ensure each portfolio adds value.

Figure 2.10. Portfolio and organisational overlaps in some parts of the system suggest room for consolidation

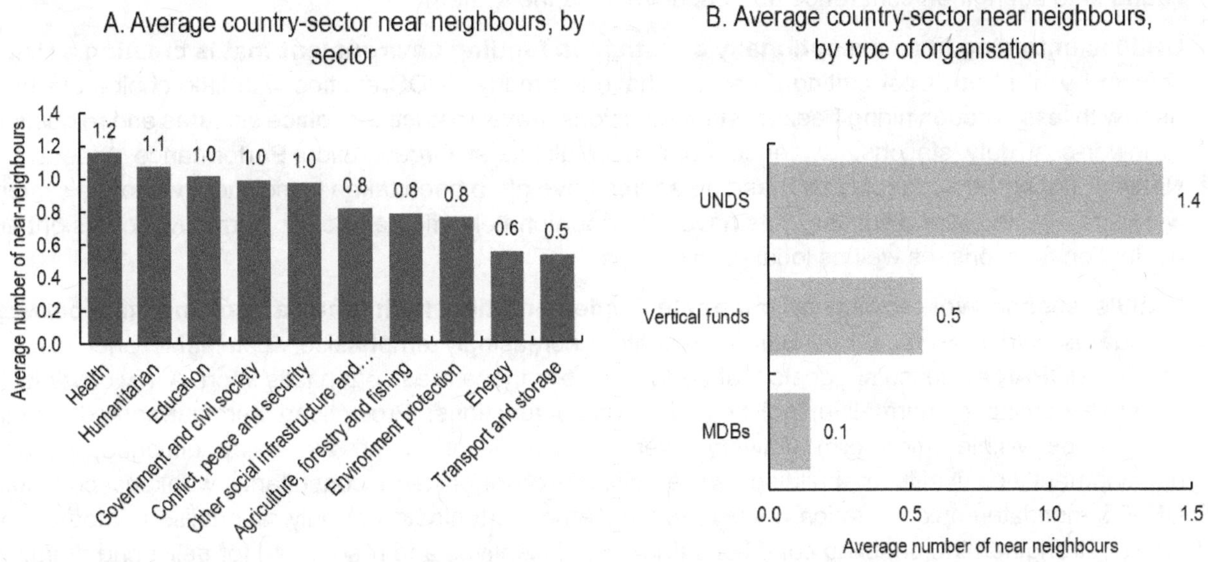

Note: Near neighbours are defined as multilateral development organisations with cosine similarity of ≥ 0.85 in their country-sector aid portfolios. Cosine similarity measures how similar two portfolios are in the distribution of their activities across countries and sectors; values range from 0 (completely different portfolios) to 1 (identical portfolios).
Source: Authors' calculations based on OECD (2026[5]), *Creditor Reporting System* (dataset), https://data-explorer.oecd.org/s/52.

Reforms already underway in the UNDS represent a constructive step towards addressing some of these structural issues. Figure 2.10, Panel B shows that UNDS entities exhibit the highest average number of country-sector near neighbours, meaning that their aid portfolios tend to overlap more frequently with those of other MDOs in the same countries and sectors. This pattern partly reflects the UNDS's co-ordination and implementation responsibilities, as well as the fact that for many years UNDS entities have been asked to deepen collaboration and "deliver as one" on the Sustainable Development Goals (SDGs). However, such calls for co-ordination were intended precisely to address existing fragmentation and overlapping engagements, not to legitimise mandate expansion in the absence of clear role differentiation. In this light, the UN80 initiative (Box 2.1) has a unique opportunity to rationalise functions within the UNDS, while also introducing greater discipline in mandate evolution by systematically assessing expansion both internally (in terms of available expertise, staffing and financial resources) and externally (in relation to other organisations' comparative advantages and system-wide coherence). Ultimately, the extent to which the UN80 initiative delivers on this potential will depend heavily on its ability to use current financial pressures to realign incentives and resources, as well as to drive structural clarification and mandate discipline. Such reforms should help MDOs refocus on areas where they add distinct value and explore opportunities for rationalising the architecture to reduce overlap and transaction costs. This may involve, where appropriate, organisational mergers or the orderly sunsetting of organisations whose mandates have become redundant or no longer reflect current development priorities, building on approaches such as the portfolio similarity analyses developed by the OECD.

Box 2.1. UN80: responding to financial pressure while revisiting long-standing structural issues

The UN80 initiative was launched by the UN Secretary-General in 2024 as a system-wide reform to respond to mounting financial pressures and address long-standing structural challenges. It is intended to provide a coherent framework for reform at a time when declining and more volatile funding, combined with expanding mandates, are testing the system's resilience. UN80 is organised around three workstreams: (i) enhancing efficiencies and operational improvements, including cost-saving measures; (ii) reviewing mandate implementation; and (iii) examining potential structural changes to strengthen coherence and impact across the system.

UN80 is unfolding in an exceptionally constrained funding environment that is creating a risk of reform by attrition. Cost-cutting pressures have left many UNDS entities with little choice but to do "less with less" through hiring freezes, staff reductions, travel restrictions, office closures and relocations to lower-cost duty stations. Evidence from the Multilateral Organisation Performance Assessment Network (MOPAN) suggests that these measures have often been taken in isolation, without a system-wide strategy. In several entities, cuts have disproportionately affected policy, normative, oversight and evaluation functions, as well as local partnerships.

UN80's second workstream on mandate implementation highlights a growing gap between mandates and results. While UN80 mandates increasingly emphasise sustainable and inclusive results, MOPAN evidence suggests that performance in these areas often falls short. A key driver is the under-resourcing of normative, policy and advisory functions. Projectised and earmarked funding incentivises visible short-term delivery over upstream work such as policy dialogue, capacity development and institution-building, while reliance on short-term consultants weakens continuity. UN80's mandate implementation review provides an opportunity to not only rationalise mandates, but also to strengthen the enabling conditions (including incentives and resources) for delivering them.

A central objective of UN80's third workstream is to strengthen intra-UN collaboration based on comparative advantage. In principle, multilateral organisations differ in their mandates, expertise, country presence and instruments. In practice, however, comparative advantage is not used systematically as an organising principle. While organisations frequently refer to their strengths in strategic documents, there is no shared framework to translate these claims into a rationalised division of labour. In addition, earmarked and competitive funding often incentivises organisations to expand their portfolios beyond their core strengths in order to secure resources and visibility. The MOPAN evidence underscores that consolidation decisions should be grounded in system-wide analyses of comparative advantage and funding arrangements that align resources with agreed divisions of labour.

Source: MOPAN (2026[23]), *Multilateral Effectiveness in a Shifting Landscape – Key Messages*, https://www.mopan.org/content/dam/mopan/en/publications/our-work/insights/thematic-briefs/key-messages/mopan-thematic-briefs-key-messages-ENG.pdf.

Together, the pressures outlined in this chapter point to a multilateral development system that delivers substantial collective value but that needs to adapt significantly to meet stakeholder expectations. Its ability to pool resources, leverage capital and operate across a wide range of risk and financing contexts has allowed it to achieve outcomes that the sum of individual donors could not deliver, a capacity of the system that has been recently reaffirmed in international commitments such as the Sevilla Commitment and the Sevilla Platform for Action. Yet, this collective value depends critically on trust in collective action and funding choices that reinforce system-wide coherence. Preventing a shift towards a low co-operation equilibrium and the subsequent erosion of the system's capacity and relevance will require more than incremental reform. It calls for resetting the system around its core principle: that multilateral action should remain greater than the sum of individual donor efforts.

Whether such a strategic reform is possible will depend both on decisions taken by donors about how and where to allocate resources, and on how MDOs themselves adapt their strategies and operational practices. The next chapter explores funding to the multilateral development system, examining recent trends in inflows, emerging vulnerabilities and the trade-offs donors face in a more constrained and politically charged multilateral development system. Chapter 4 then turns to the multilateral development organisations, assessing how their institutional behaviours, reform choices and delivery models will shape the system's capacity to respond to current and future development challenges.

References

African Development Fund (2025), *ADF-17 Replenishment: In historic move, African countries race to contribute to continent's development*, https://adf.afdb.org/adf-17-replenishment-in-historic-move-african-countries-race-to-contribute-to-continents-development/. [6]

Banga, A. (2025), *Development is how we compete, grow, and stay secure*, https://blogs.worldbank.org/en/voices/development-is-how-we-compete-grow-and-stay-secure. [17]

Bridgetown Initiative (2022), *Bridgetown Initiative on the Reform of the International Development and Climate Finance Architecture*, https://www.bridgetown-initiative.org/. [16]

Government of Canada (2026), *Davos 2026: Special address by Mark Carney, Prime Minister of Canada*, https://www.weforum.org/stories/2026/01/davos-2026-special-address-by-mark-carney-prime-minister-of-canada/. [12]

Government of the United States (2026), *Withdrawing the United States from International Organizations, Conventions and Treaties that are Contrary to the Interests of the United States*, https://www.whitehouse.gov/presidential-actions/2026/01/withdrawing-the-united-states-from-international-organizations-conventions-and-treaties-that-are-contrary-to-the-interests-of-the-united-states/. [10]

Graham, E. (2017), "Follow the money: How trends in financing are changing governance at international organizations", *Global Policy*, Vol. 8/S5, pp. 15–25, https://onlinelibrary.wiley.com/doi/full/10.1111/1758-5899.12450. [3]

Ihl, J. et al. (2025), "The effectiveness of core and earmarked funding in multilateral development cooperation: Systematic review", *DEval Discussion Paper*, Vol. 02/2025, https://www.deval.org/fileadmin/Redaktion/PDF/05-Publikationen/Berichte/2025_Multilaterale_EZ/DEval-DP-02-2025-MultilateralDC-Web.pdf. [2]

MOPAN (2026), *Beyond Overlaps: Leveraging Comparative Advantage for Multilateral Collaboration*, Multilateral Organisation Performance Assessment Network, Paris, https://www.mopan.org/en/our-work/performance-insights/multilateral-effectiveness-in-a-shifting-landscape/comparative-advantage-un80-summary.html. [7]

MOPAN (2026), *Multilateral Effectiveness in a Shifting Landscape - Key Messages*, Multilateral Organisation Performance Assessment Network, Paris, https://www.mopan.org/content/dam/mopan/en/publications/our-work/insights/thematic-briefs/key-messages/mopan-thematic-briefs-key-messages-ENG.pdf. [23]

OECD (2026), *Creditor Reporting System (dataset)*, https://data-explorer.oecd.org/s/52 (accessed on 15 January 2026). [5]

OECD (2026), *List of ODA-eligible international organisations*, https://webfs.oecd.org/oda/DataCollection/Resources/OECD-ODA-Single-Table-2026-for-2025-flows.xlsx. [1]

OECD (2026), *Providers' Total Use of the Multilateral System (dataset)*, http://data-explorer.oecd.org/s/1td (accessed on 22 February 2026). [15]

OECD (2025), “Cuts in official development assistance: OECD projections for 2025 and the near term”, *OECD Policy Briefs*, No. 26, OECD Publishing, Paris, https://doi.org/10.1787/8c530629-en. [14]

OECD (2024), *Multilateral Development Finance 2024*, OECD Publishing, Paris, https://doi.org/10.1787/8f1e2b9b-en. [4]

OECD (2020), *Multilateral Development Finance 2020*, OECD Publishing, Paris, https://doi.org/10.1787/e61fdf00-en. [11]

OECD/UNDP (forthcoming), *Making Development Co-operation More Effective - 2026 Progress Report*. [9]

UNGA (2025), *Resolutions Adopted by the General Assembly on 30 December 2025*, United Nations General Assembly, New York, https://docs.un.org/en/A/RES/80/244%20A-C. [22]

UNGA (2024), *Resolutions Adopted by the General Assembly on 24 December 2024*, United Nations General Assembly, New York, https://digitallibrary.un.org/record/4071044?ln=en&v=pdf. [21]

United Nations (2025), *Sevilla Commitment. Fourth International Conference on Financing for Development*, https://financing.desa.un.org/sites/default/files/2025-08/FFD4%20Outcome%20Booklet%20v4_EN%20-%20spread.pdf. [8]

United Nations (2025), *Sevilla Platform for Action*, https://financing.desa.un.org/ffd4/sevilla-platform-action. [13]

United Nations (2025), “United Nations revises 2026 regular budget proposal, pairing cost reductions with initial reform measures”, *UN News*, https://news.un.org/en/story/2025/09/1165850. [20]

World Bank (2024), *FY25 World Bank Budget*, World Bank, Washington D.C., https://documents1.worldbank.org/curated/en/099080824144031957/pdf/BOSIB196bde0ea0fb1b88215cf5c0e36a36.pdf. [19]

World Bank Group (2025), “De-risking development: All you need to know about guarantees”, *The Development Podcast*, https://www.worldbank.org/en/news/podcast/2025/07/03/de-risking-guarantees-miga-development-podcast. [18]

3 Funding to the multilateral development system

This chapter analyses inflows to the multilateral development system, exploring the implications for the system of recent ODA cuts announced by major donors. It documents the sharp reversal of multilateral funding growth in 2024 and shows that the system's exposure stems in part from its reliance on a small group of major donors, several of whom have announced substantial ODA cuts. The implications include unavoidable trade-offs between scale and concessionality, and a heightened risk of earmarked funding displacing rather than complementing core contributions, weakening the financial foundations of multilateral effectiveness at a time when the system is needed most. Finally, the chapter shows how organisations' vulnerability differs depending on their funding models, the balance between funding modalities, donor concentration and the diversification of the donor base.

3.1. After years of expansion, funding to the multilateral development system has reached a turning point

3.1.1. Funding to the multilateral development system is in decline

After several years of steady growth, funding to the multilateral development system reversed course in 2024, reflecting mounting fiscal and political pressures in donor countries. Although core and earmarked contributions to multilateral development organisations continued to increase through 2023 to reach a USD 107.6 billion all-time-high – supported by a temporary rebound in core funding following the pandemic – in 2024, both core and earmarked contributions declined sharply, bringing total multilateral contributions down to USD 91.3 billion (a 15% fall) (Figure 3.1, Panel A). The contraction in total inflows was driven mainly by reduced funding to UNDS entities, vertical funds and international financial institutions (IFIs), including the World Bank Group and the International Monetary Fund (Figure 3.1, Panel B).

This decline in funding to the multilateral system mirrors the global contraction observed in total official development assistance. Unlike previous episodes of volatility driven by exceptional shocks, such as the 5% decline in core contributions observed in 2022 (coinciding with the COVID-19 pandemic and the war in Ukraine), the current downturn reflects deeper structural pressures on aid budgets. As a result, the decline observed in 2024 is more likely to be the start of a medium-term trend, rather than a short-lived fluctuation in ODA volumes. The simultaneous and substantial funding cuts announced by one-third of DAC members in 2025 (discussed in Section 2.2.2) are unprecedented in recent decades, and most of the cutters have announced further reductions through 2027, as discussed later in this section (OECD, 2025[1]).

Figure 3.1. Contributions to the multilateral system declined by 15% in 2024

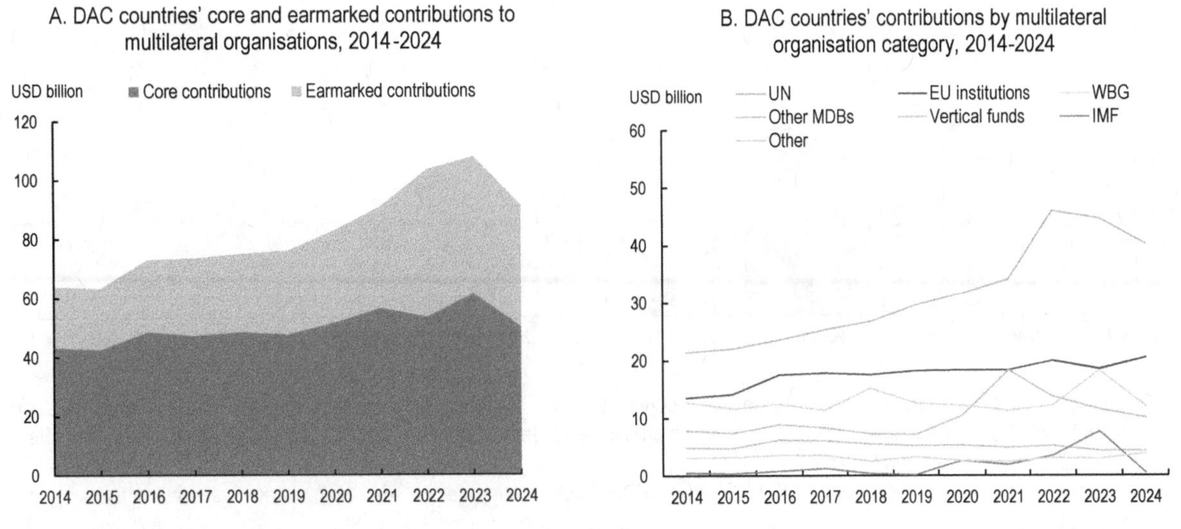

Note: Calculations are based on disbursements, in 2023 constant prices.
Source: Authors' calculations based on OECD (2026[2]), *Providers' Total Use of the Multilateral System* (dataset), http://data-explorer.oecd.org/s/1td.

The extent of the funding drop over 2023-2024 differed across categories of multilateral organisations. Funding to the UNDS declined in 2023 and 2024 following a decade of gradual expansion that peaked in 2022. The 2022 peak was driven partly by a surge in crisis-related funding, notably in response to Russia's war of aggression against Ukraine. As Figure 3.1, Panel B shows, total funding to the UNDS decreased by 2.8% in 2023, and by 9.8% in 2024, down to USD 40.2 billion, affecting both core and earmarked contributions. The sharp fall in 2024 contributions was driven by a 19% fall in Ukraine funding, while the gradual decline of non-Ukraine funding starting as early as 2022 (Figure 3.2, Panel A).

Recent trends in funding to vertical funds illustrate how these issue-specific mechanisms can scale up rapidly in response to shocks, but also how exposed they are to shifting priorities and fiscal tightening. Funding to health-focused vertical funds – Gavi and The Global Fund to Fight AIDS, Tuberculosis and Malaria – peaked in 2021 and 2022, reflecting the surge in resources mobilised in response to the COVID-19 pandemic (Figure 3.2, Panel B). In 2023 and 2024, this expansion slowed down, with inflows declining as emergency financing needs receded and donor attention shifted to other priorities. Environment and climate-related vertical funds – the Green Climate Fund (GCF) and the Global Environment Facility (GEF) – show a different pattern, with funding continuing to rise until 2023, before declining in 2024. This downturn coincided with the broader contraction in multilateral funding and reflects, in part, changes in the policy priorities of some donors alongside tighter budgetary conditions.

For the World Bank Group and the IMF, their 2024 decline largely reflects the unwinding of exceptionally high contribution levels recorded in 2023 (Figure 3.1, Panel B), which coincided with major replenishment cycles: IDA20 for the World Bank Group, and the launch and inaugural capitalisation of the Resilience and Sustainability Trust (RST) at the IMF. In contrast, funding to the European Union institutions increased over the same period, from USD 18.4 to USD 20.5 billion.

Figure 3.2. Tapering crisis response, tightening aid budgets and evolving donor priorities drove the recent drop in multilateral funding

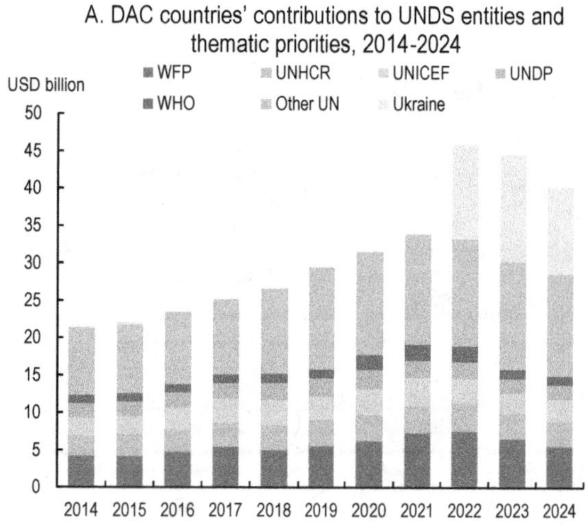

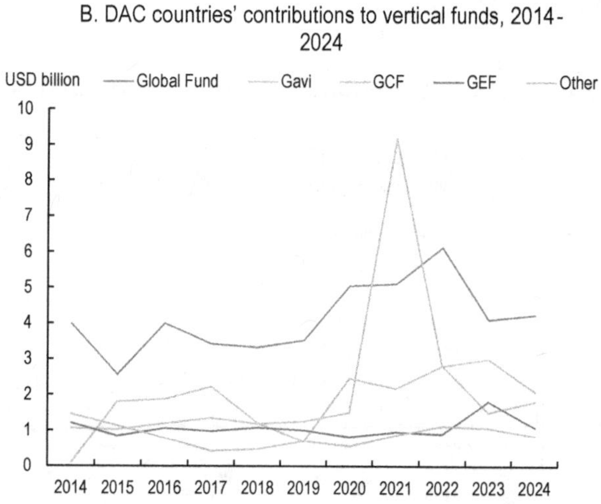

Note: Calculations are based on disbursements, in 2023 constant prices. In Panel A, contributions to specific UNDS entities exclude disbursements for which Ukraine is the recipient country, which are lumped together under the "Ukraine" category. The Global Fund=The Global Fund to Fight AIDS, Tuberculosis and Malaria.

Source: Authors' calculations based on OECD (2026[2]), Providers' *Total Use of the Multilateral System* (dataset), http://data-explorer.oecd.org/s/1td.

The funding decline is set to continue

Projections suggest that multilateral contributions could decline further if the aid cuts announced by donors are implemented as planned. The projections shown in Figure 3.3 are derived from a survey which asked DAC members about their recent and expected reductions in their total ODA budgets over the coming years (OECD, 2025[1]). To translate these expected reductions into a forward-looking scenario for multilateral funding, the analysis assumes that each donor maintains a constant share of multilateral contributions within its overall ODA envelope. Under this assumption, total contributions to the multilateral development system are projected to decline by approximately 23% to 30% between 2023 and 2027. This shows that MDOs will face a deteriorating funding environment even in the absence of deliberate policy decisions to scale back multilateral engagement.

Figure 3.3. Contributions to the multilateral development system are set to continue falling

DAC members' total contributions to the multilateral system, 2010-2024 and projections

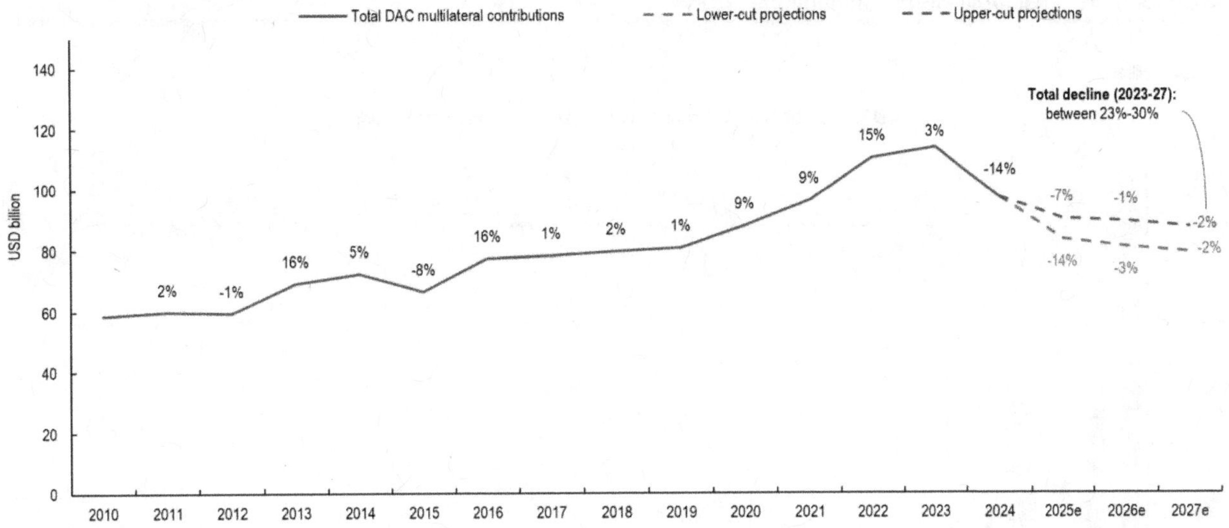

Note: Calculations are based on disbursements, in 2023 constant prices. Projections are generated by applying each donor's ODA percentage change, as estimated in (OECD, 2025[1]), to their respective multilateral contributions.

Source: Authors' calculations based on OECD (2026[2]), *Providers' Total Use of the Multilateral System* (dataset), http://data-explorer.oecd.org/s/1td; and OECD (2025[1]), "Cuts in official development assistance: OECD projections for 2025 and the near term", https://doi.org/10.1787/8c530629-en.

A significant share of multilateral development organisations have already had funding reductions confirmed by their donors. While the projections in Figure 3.3 provide a perspective on the overall potential impact of the announced budget cuts, they only capture one side of the picture. A complementary perspective emerges when looking at the expectations of MDOs themselves. Evidence from a recent survey among MDOs indicates that most of them have received formal donor notices of funding reductions (MOPAN, 2025[3]). Across the 18 respondents that responded to the question, 15 indicated they had received formal notice of funding reductions from donors. In addition, one-third of the respondents (6) estimated the scale of their funding reduction for their next budget or replenishment to be within a range of 21% to 30% lower relative to the previous budget. When considered in conjunction with the donors' own projections, these MDO expectations suggest that the multilateral development system is entering a period of significant, and potentially sustained, funding contraction.

The severity and concurrence of the projected declines in multilateral contributions raise concerns about the system's ability to plan for and absorb the resulting shock. Beyond their scale, these projected cuts also matter because of how they are likely to be implemented: in a constrained environment, pressures to preserve visibility or maintain specific priorities may increasingly shape decisions about funding modalities and allocation choices. This raises questions not only about the overall volume of resources flowing to the multilateral development system, but also about the balance between core and earmarked funding – a topic which is turned to in Section 3.1.3.

3.1.2. Heavy reliance on a few DAC donors leaves the system highly exposed

The heavy dependence of the multilateral development system on a small number of DAC providers has implications for both the stability and the vulnerability of the system. In 2024, four countries accounted for about half of total DAC contributions to the multilateral development system: the United States, Germany, France and the United Kingdom (Figure 3.4). As a result, funding decisions of a handful donors have system-wide implications for the multilateral development system.

Figure 3.4. Four countries accounted for half of DAC members' multilateral contributions in 2024

DAC members' total multilateral contributions, 2024

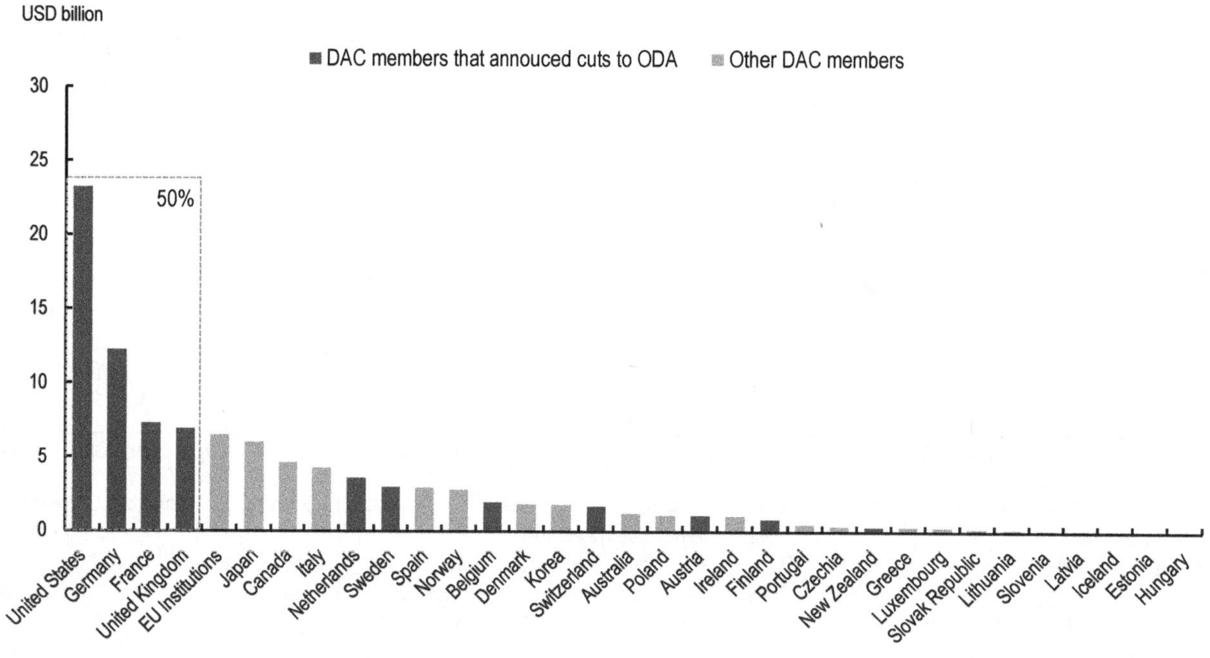

Note: Calculations are based on disbursements, in 2023 constant prices.
Source: Authors' calculations based on OECD (2026[2]), *Providers' Total Use of the Multilateral System* (dataset), http://data-explorer.oecd.org/s/1td.

Aid cuts announced by the system's top donors have exposed the risks this dependence creates. Importantly, the exposure of the multilateral development system is amplified by the fact that the four largest DAC contributors are all among those that have announced reductions to their ODA budgets (Section 3.1.1). As a result, the current funding downturn is not only broad-based but is also concentrated among those donors whose decisions carry the greatest weight for the system as a whole, increasing the risk of abrupt impacts on MDOs' financial capacity and planning. As shown in Figure 3.5, a significant share of multilateral funding currently comes from these and the other seven DAC members that have announced or are already implementing cuts to their ODA, suggesting that the impact on multilateral development finance is likely to be both substantial and widespread. Section 3.2.3 outlines some ways in which MDOs can broaden their funding bases.

Figure 3.5. The 11 DAC members that have announced aid cuts account for a significant share of major MDOs' total funding

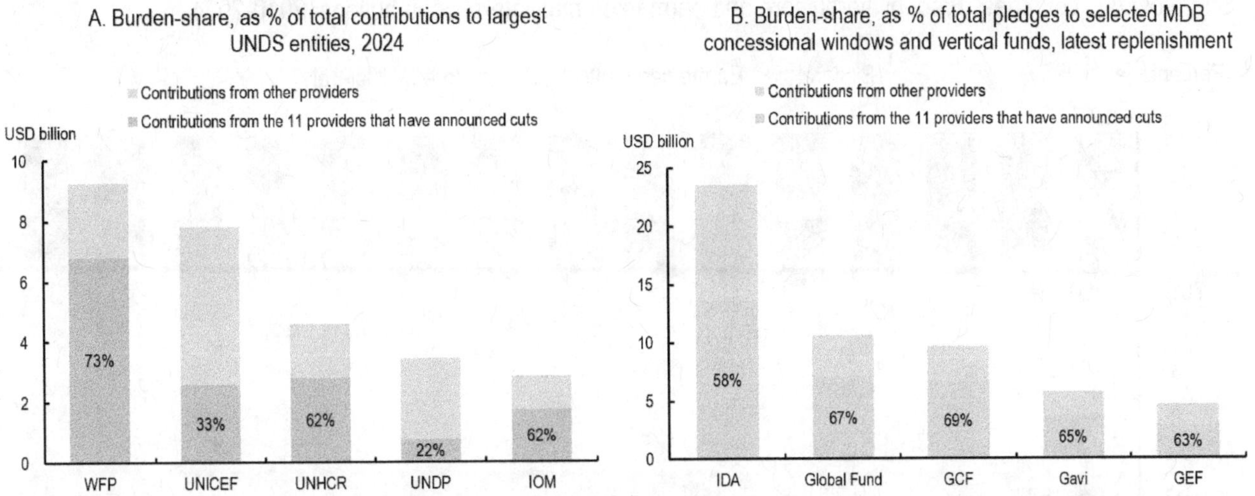

Source: Calculations for Panel A are based on a dataset of donor contributions to the United Nations Development System (UNDS) provided directly by United Nations Department of Economic and Social Affairs (UNDESA). It excludes local contributions (i.e. funding provided by a government to UN activities implemented in its own country) from analysis. Calculations for Panel B are based on the latest completed replenishments for those multilateral funds for which full contributions data are available: IDA20, Global Fund-7, Global Climate Fund (GCF) Second Formal Replenishment, Gavi 2021-2025 and Global Environment Facility (GEF-8). Not all ODA providers that have announced cuts to ODA for 2025-27 participate in all the multilateral funds analysed here.

3.1.3. Core contributions continue to lose out to earmarked funding

Earmarked funding has shifted from substituting bilateral aid to increasingly displacing core contributions in DAC members' total ODA

For much of the 2010s, earmarking largely expanded at the expense of direct bilateral aid, while core contributions remained comparatively stable as a share of DAC members' total ODA. Between 2010 and 2021, the share of direct bilateral aid in DAC members' ODA declined from 63% to 55%, while earmarked multilateral funding rose from 11% to 17% (Figure 3.6). Over that same period, core multilateral funding remained close to its long-run range, at around 27% of total ODA. Although this increase in earmarked contributions was not without consequences for the system's effectiveness (e.g. increasing fragmentation), on the whole the core funding base underpinning multilateral mandates was not directly impacted.

Recent shifts suggest earmarked funding may increasingly displace core multilateral funding in DAC members' total ODA. Since 2020, the relationship between direct bilateral aid, earmarked and core funding has evolved, as spikes in earmarking have coincided with sharper dips in core funding. Figure 3.6 shows that earmarked contributions increased from 17% of DAC members' total ODA in 2021 to 21% in 2022, before going back to 19% and 18% in 2023 and 2024 respectively. Meanwhile, the share of core multilateral funding, which had remained constant at around 27% between 2010 and 2021, fell to 23% in 2024. The implications of these recent shifts for the multilateral development system are discussed in Section 3.2.2.

Figure 3.6. Bilateral and earmarked multilateral contributions are rising at the expense of core contributions

Share of DAC countries' direct bilateral, core and earmarked multilateral contributions, 2010-2024

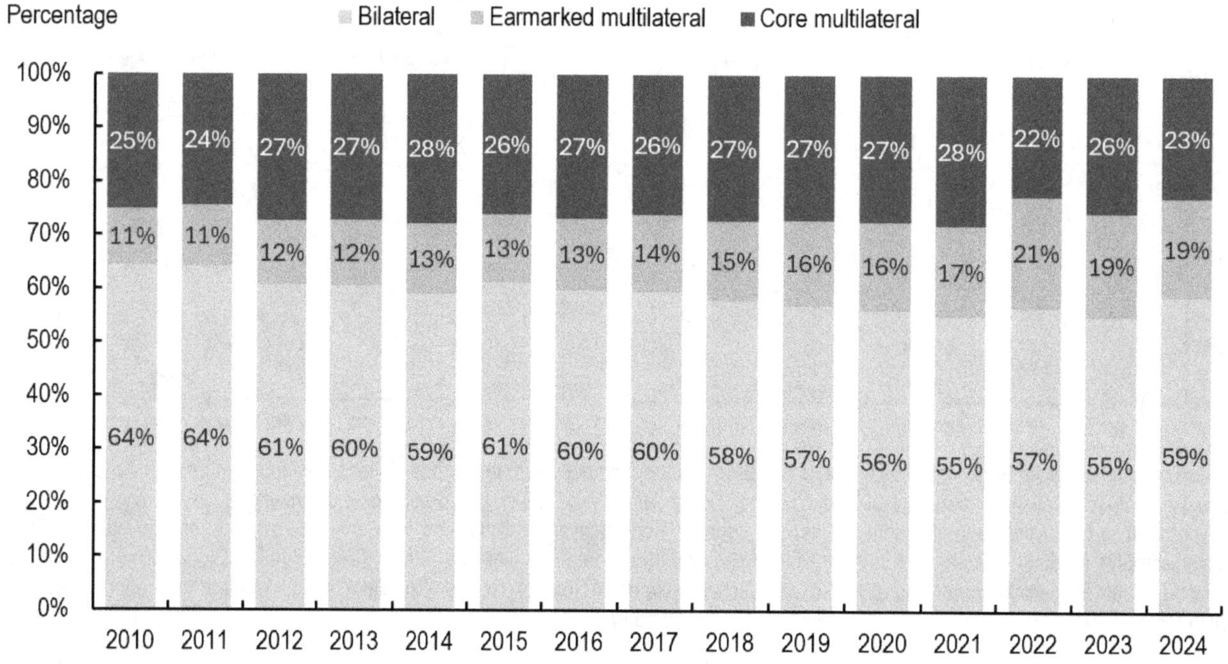

Note: Direct bilateral ODA refers to DAC members' bilateral ODA excluding earmarked contributions (multi-bi aid). Calculations are based on gross disbursements in 2023 constant prices.
Source: Authors' calculations based on OECD (2026[4]), *DAC1: Flows by Provider (ODA+OOF+Private)* (dataset), http://data-explorer.oecd.org/s/9w.

Multilateral development organisations receive a growing share of contributions in the form of earmarked resources, but patterns vary across DAC members

The evolution of earmarking within multilateral contributions confirms their growing importance in the funding mix of the system. After experiencing a period of slow but steady growth from 2010 to 2021, the share of DAC countries' earmarked contributions to multilateral organisations peaked in 2022 (at 48% of DAC members' total multilateral contributions) amid exceptional crisis-related financing linked to the COVID-19 pandemic and the war in Ukraine (Figure 3.7). It then briefly declined in 2023 to 43% of total contributions – reflecting a decline of earmarked funding for the COVID-19 response and a moderate rebound in core contributions – before rising again in 2024 to 45%, its second highest level on record.

Figure 3.7. Earmarked contributions continue to increase as a share of total multilateral contributions

Share of DAC countries' earmarked contributions to multilateral organisations, 2014-2024

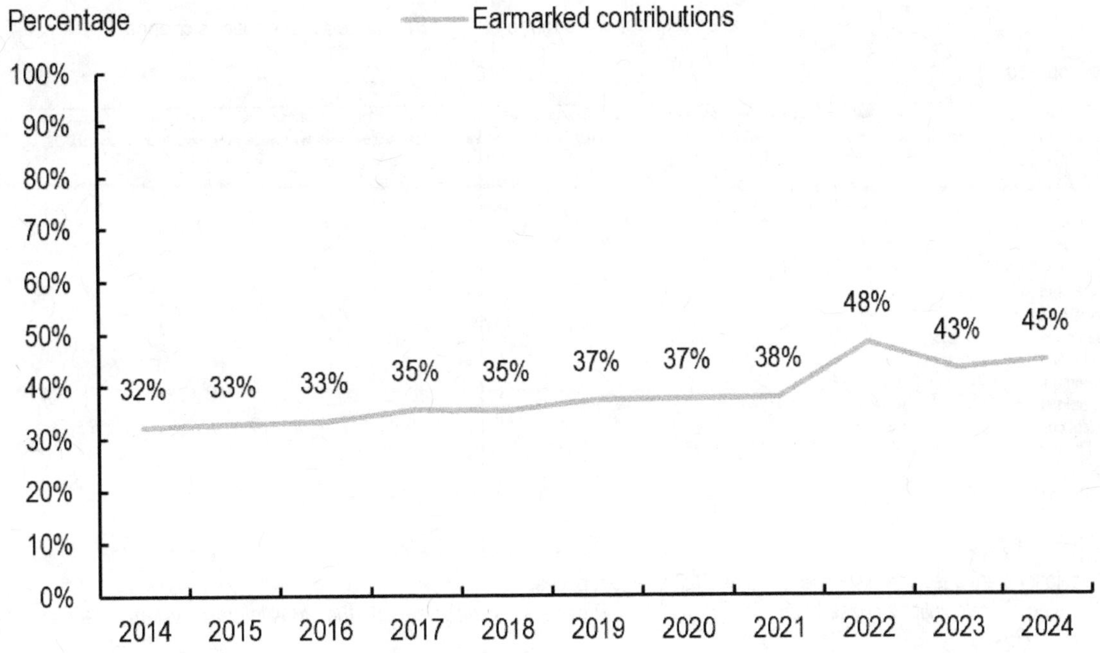

Note: Calculations are based on disbursements, in 2023 constant prices.
Source: Authors' calculations based on OECD (2026[2]), *Providers' Total Use of the Multilateral System* (dataset), http://data-explorer.oecd.org/s/1td.

DAC members differ markedly in how they adjust the balance between core and earmarked funding. Year-on-year changes in core and earmarked contributions show significantly more variation across donors in 2024 than in previous years. The most dramatic differences in approach are those by the United States and Germany – the two largest contributors to the multilateral system (Figure 3.8). In 2024, the United States reduced its core contributions by USD 7.3 billion while expanding its earmarked flows by USD 9.4 billion, largely driven by increased support to Ukraine. On the other hand, Germany increased its core contributions by USD 7.5 billion while reducing earmarked funding by USD 9.2 billion. These divergent approaches are shaped by domestic political considerations, budgetary processes and strategic preferences regarding the role of multilateral organisations. At the same time, they reflect a broader environment of heightened uncertainty and limited co-ordination across the system, as funding decisions remain primarily shaped by national budget processes and domestic political considerations, with adjustments made largely at the national level. The result is an increasingly fragmented and uncertain multilateral funding landscape.

Figure 3.8. Changes in core and earmarked contributions show contrasting adjustment patterns across DAC donors

Change in DAC members' total use of the multilateral development system (top 20 members showing the largest change), 2021-2022 contributions versus 2023-2024 contributions

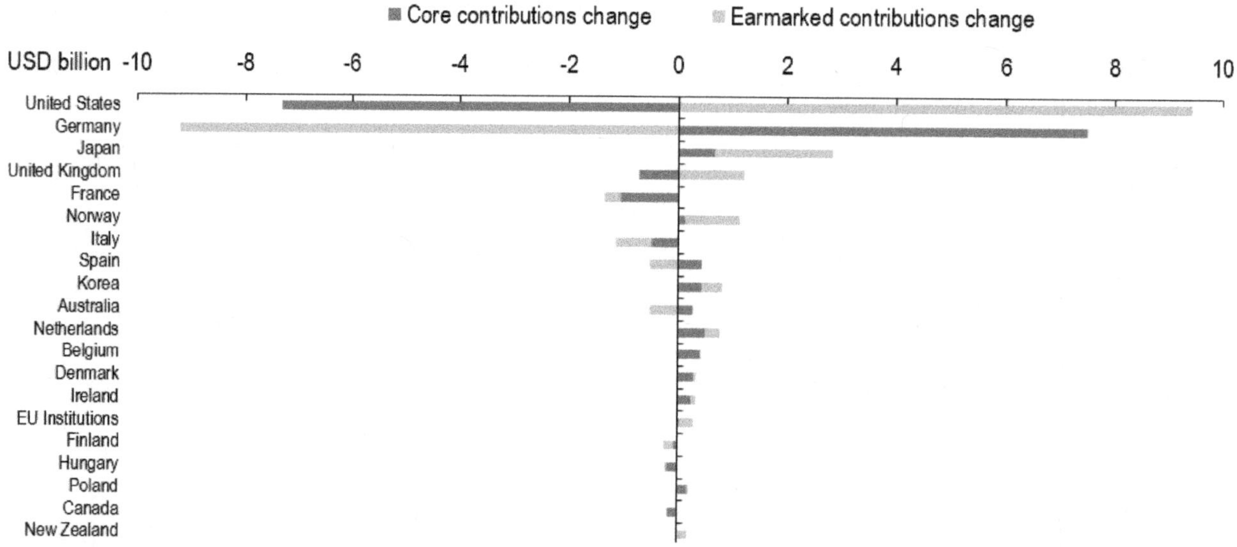

Note: Calculations are based on disbursements, in 2023 constant prices.
Source: Authors' calculations based on OECD (2026[2]),Providers' *Total Use of the Multilateral System* (dataset), http://data-explorer.oecd.org/s/1td.

Despite the overall trend towards rising earmarking, several DAC members continue to demonstrate a strong commitment to core funding. In 2024, 24 out of 32 DAC countries, accounting for roughly 60% of total multilateral contributions, provided core contributions exceeding what would be expected based on their share of DAC gross national income (GNI). Nordic and Benelux countries continue to feature prominently in this group, reflecting a sustained commitment to providing predictable and flexible funding to the multilateral system (Figure 3.9). Together, these countries account for seven of the top ten positions for core contributions relative to DAC GNI.

Figure 3.9. Nordic and Benelux countries provide significantly more than their "fair share" of core funding to the multilateral system

Core contributions to multilateral organisations relative to countries' share in the overall DAC GNI, 2022-2024

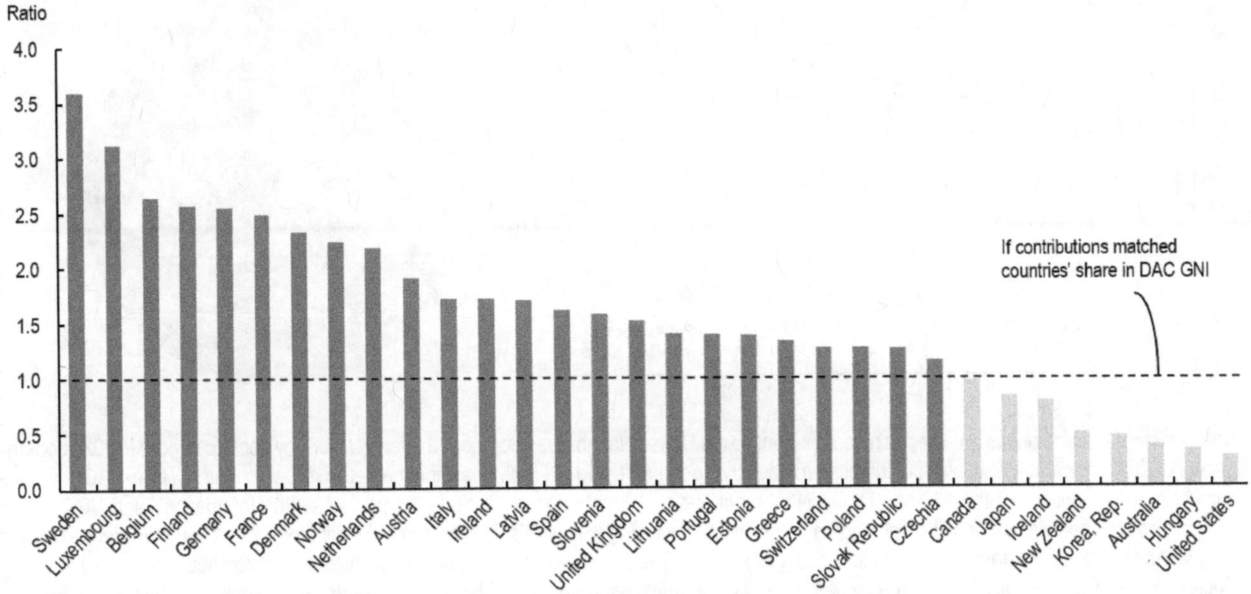

Note: Calculations are based on disbursements, in 2023 constant prices.
Source: Authors' calculations based on OECD (2026[2]), *Providers' Total Use of the Multilateral System* (dataset), http://data-explorer.oecd.org/s/1td.

3.1.4. Tightening budgets among the system's traditional donors may open space for emerging donors to play a greater role

In the last decade, there has been limited success in crowding in emerging donors and diversifying the UNDS' donor base. For years, UN funding experts have called for a broadening of the UNDS's donor base beyond a handful of DAC members (Dag Hammarskjöld Foundation; UN MPTFO, 2017[5]). Yet even accounting for the recent contraction, DAC countries' contributions have risen strongly over the past decade, increasing from USD 23.3 billion in 2014 to 29.5 billion in 2024 (Figure 3.10, Panel A), raising their share in total funding to the UNDS from 65% in 2014 to 69% in 2024 (Figure 3.10, Panel B). In contrast, emerging donors – defined loosely as non-DAC countries and private donors (i.e. private sector, foundations and NGOs) – have seen a downward funding trend. Over the same period, the combined contributions of the 162 non-DAC UN member states fell from USD 2.6 to 2.3 billion, an 11% reduction, driven notably by significant declines in contributions by Saudi Arabia (-60%) and Kuwait (-85%). Total private funding declined from USD 4.6 to 3.8 billion, an 18% fall. These declines brought non-DAC countries' funding share down from 7% to 5%, while the private donor share declined even more, from 13% to 9%.

Figure 3.10. DAC countries' UNDS contributions rose steadily over 2014-2024, while emerging donor contributions have weakened

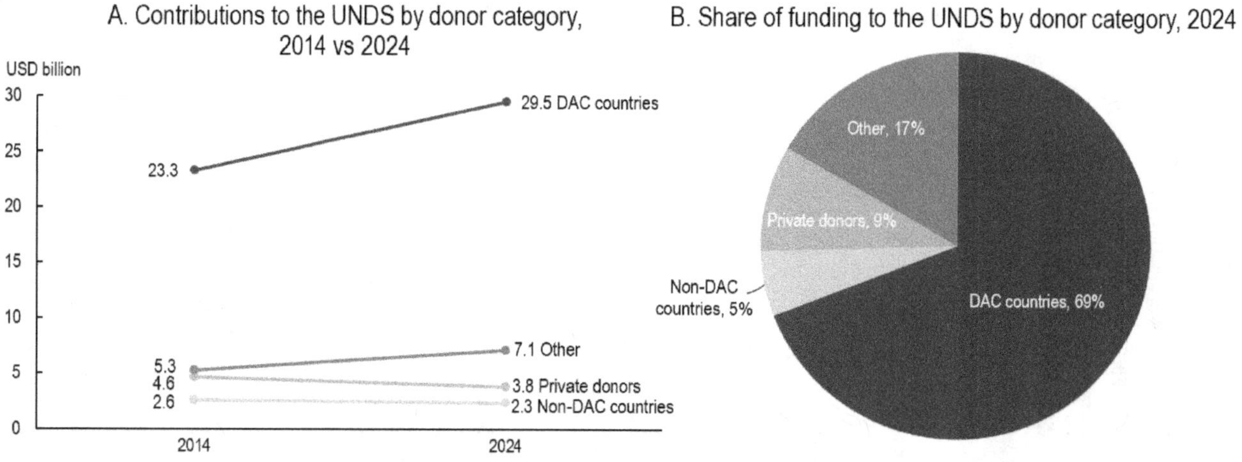

Note: In Panel A, calculations are based on contributions to the United Nations Development System (UNDS) by donor category in 2024 constant prices, excluding local contributions (i.e. funding provided by a government to UN activities implemented in its own country). "Non-DAC countries" capture the contributions of the 162 non-DAC UN member states. "Private donors" include the private sector, foundations and NGOs, while "Other" primarily contains the multilateral funders of the UNDS, including IFIs, vertical funds and EU Institutions. The chart compares 2014 with 2024 contributions due to data constraints for other years. Panel B is also based on 2024 prices, excluding local contributions.
Source: Authors' calculations based on a dataset of donor contributions to the United Nations Development System (UNDS) provided directly by the United Nations Department of Economic and Social Affairs (UNDESA).

The decline of emerging donor funding to the UNDS underscores the urgency of strengthening efforts to diversify the UN system's funding base. The UNDS still depends on DAC donors for 69% of total funding (77% when we include European Commission contributions), a vulnerability that has been exposed by the current wave of correlated DAC donor cuts. Reversing the slowdown in emerging donor funding could help reduce this dependence on DAC donors over time. Strengthening this diversification drive will be important both to weather the current aid crisis and to build resilience to future shocks.

Despite the overall downward trend in non-DAC government contributions, there have been some notable increases by some countries. The People's Republic of China quadrupled its funding to the UNDS between 2014 and 2024, making it the fastest-growing contributor of the top 20 government donors in 2014. It jumped three positions in the ranking of non-DAC government donors to the UNDS, becoming by far the biggest non-DAC donor in 2024 (Figure 3.11). While Saudi Arabia and Kuwait retreated as the top two donors in 2014, two other Gulf States, the UAE and Qatar, jumped two and six positions respectively. India also accelerated its contributions, rising six places and re-establishing itself among the top five non-DAC contributors.

Figure 3.11. China, the UAE, Qatar and India have risen up the ranks of leading non-DAC donors to the UNDS

Top 10 non-DAC government donors to the UNDS in 2024, with arrows indicating change in rank relative to 2014

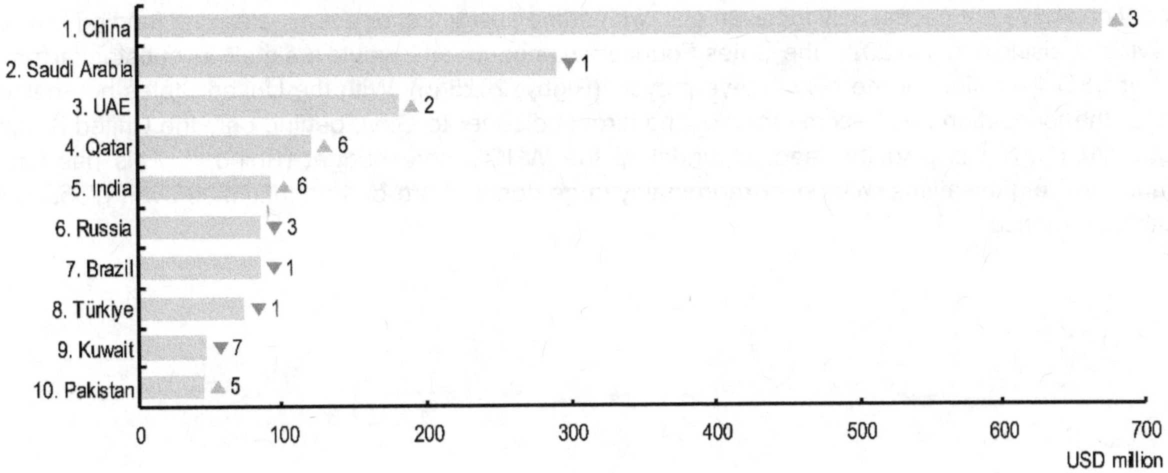

Note: Local contributions (i.e. funding provided by a government to UN activities implemented in its own country) are excluded from analysis.
Source: Authors' calculations based on a dataset of donor contributions to the United Nations Development System (UNDS) provided directly by the United Nations Department of Economic and Social Affairs (UNDESA).

While non-DAC countries are small system-wide donors, they can be important funders at the entity level. For example, in 2024 amid the humanitarian crisis in Gaza, Saudi Arabia boosted its funding to the United Nations Relief and Works Agency for Palestine Refugees in the Near East (UNRWA) by 140% relative to 2023, becoming its sixth largest government donor that year. From 2018 to 2023 when the United States were out of UNESCO (rejoined mid-2023), China was the leading donor to the entity, providing a financial lifeline to the budget-constrained organisation (see Section 3.2.3 for further details on UNESCO's navigation of budget cuts). As highlighted in the last edition of the Multilateral Development Finance report, such targeted support to regions, themes and entities can boost emerging donors' influence in select organisations (OECD, 2024[6]). For example, shortly after the US withdrawal from UNESCO in 2017, and the resulting jump in China's share of funding, a Chinese official was appointed Deputy Director General, the organisation's second most senior leadership position (UNESCO, 2018[7]).

The recent aid pullback by the multilateral system's traditional donors could accelerate changes in donor patterns in other parts of the system, with IDA's recent replenishment a case in point. For IDA's 20th replenishment, negotiated in 2021, France, Germany, Japan, the United Kingdom and the United States pledged the largest amounts by far (Martinez and Landers, 2025[8]). At IDA21 in 2025, all these top donors, except for the United Kingdom, reduced their pledges compared to the previous replenishment. China, meanwhile, boosted its pledge by 14% in nominal terms compared to the last cycle, becoming a top five pledger to an IDA replenishment for the first time in history. This is a remarkable rise, considering China was only 20th largest pledger as recently as IDA16, which was completed in 2010 (Martinez and Estes, 2025[9]).

Shifting aid dynamics are also prompting African countries to rethink their role as investors in regional development via the African Development Bank (AfDB). Until recently, African countries contributing to the African Development Fund (ADF, AfDB's concessional window) was a rare occurrence, with only four African countries pledging at ADF16 (African Center for Economic Transformation, 2025[10]).

At the ADF's 17th replenishment, concluded in 2025, however, an additional 19 African countries pledged funding for the first time (African Development Fund, 2025[11]).

Amid traditional donor pull-back, the Gates Foundation has also become a dominant funder of specific multilateral organisations, especially in the health sector. While several large DAC donors have simultaneously decided to cut ODA over 2025-27, non-official donors such as the private sector and foundations have not necessarily followed suit, with some sustaining or even increasing funding levels. At a Gavi fundraising event in 2025, the Gates Foundation announced it would maintain its substantial funding level at USD 1.6 billion for the next five-year cycle (Rigby, 2025[12]). With the United States not making a pledge, the foundation has become the second largest pledger to Gavi, behind only the United Kingdom (Rigby, 2025[12]). It is also the leading funder of the WHO's core budget (Box 3.1). This has left the philanthropic organisations with an extraordinarily large donor share of, and influence over, global public health governance.

Box 3.1. The World Health Organization's evolving funding structure

The evolving funding mix of the World Health Organization (WHO) illustrates how the global aid crisis can accelerate shifts in donor composition, including increasing dependence on philanthropic donors. As several traditional public donors have reduced their contributions, non-official donors now account for a growing share of WHO's resources. The ranking of largest contributors to WHO's core budget shows private and philanthropic actors such as the Gates Foundation (1st) and Rotary International (9th) among the largest funders (Figure 3.12). In addition to becoming the single largest donor to WHO's core budget in 2024-2025, the Gates Foundation is a leading donor to Gavi, itself a major funder of WHO (3rd) and a major global health provider. Given the United States' withdrawal from WHO and Gavi in 2025, the foundation's funding share is likely to rise further, giving it unprecedented leverage over global public health governance.

Greater reliance on non-official funding sources introduces new dynamics into multilateral financing, including differences in funding predictability, accountability arrangements and decision-making processes. Over time, these changes have the potential to influence priority-setting, governance dynamics and the balance between collectively agreed mandates and donor-driven preferences, with implications for how multilateral organisations define and pursue their core functions.

Figure 3.12. The Gates Foundation has replaced the United States as the leading donor to the World Health Organization's programme budget

Disbursements to WHO's programme budget, 2024-2025, USD million

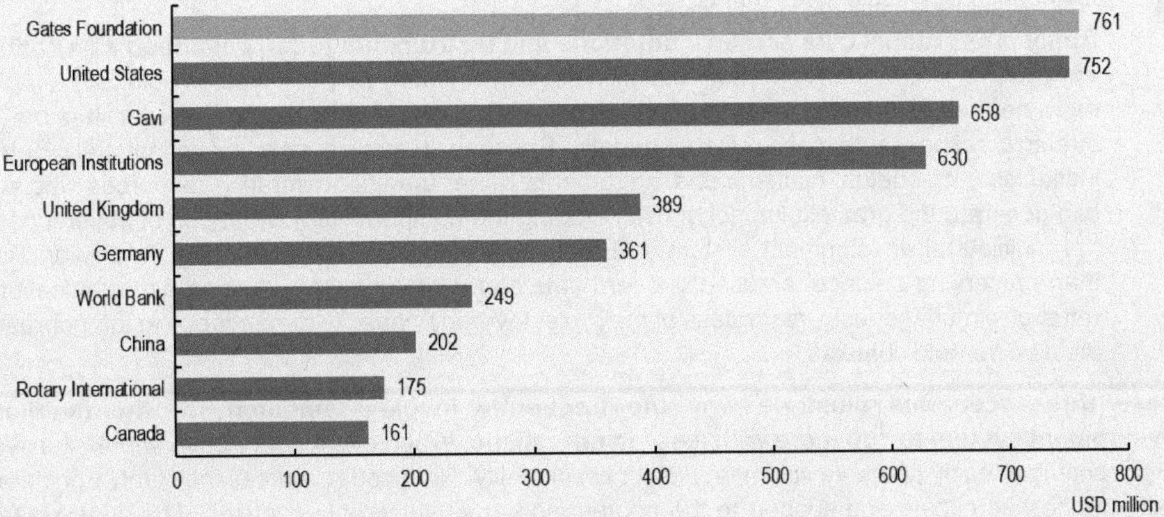

Note: In 2024, the programme budget accounted for 79% of the WHO's total revenue.
Sources: World Health Organization (2026[13]), *Contributors* (dataset), https://open.who.int/2024-25/contributors/contributor; World Health Organization (2025[14]), *Audited Financial Statements for the Year Ended 2024*, https://apps.who.int/gb/ebwha/pdf_files/WHA78/A78_18-en.pdf.

These trends and shifts in volumes, funding modalities and donor composition also point to deeper structural pressures within the multilateral funding model. The next section examines the implications of these trends, exploring how tightening budgets and shifting donor behaviour may reshape funding patterns, intensify trade-offs, and affect the stability and predictability of resources entering the multilateral development system.

3.2. What constrained aid budgets mean for the multilateral development system

3.2.1. In a context of shrinking funding, donors face difficult trade-offs

Tightening aid budgets are forcing donors to make difficult choices about how to use limited resources. A reduction in donor contributions can translate into markedly different outcomes for the composition, scale and impact of multilateral outflows depending on how donors prioritise competing objectives and allocate funding. Figure 3.13 illustrates these trade-offs using a stylised simulation based on a hypothetical yet plausible 15% reduction in DAC donor contributions to the multilateral system, consistent with the projections presented in Section 3.1.2. It shows three options:

1. **Safeguard overall multilateral output by prioritising leverage mechanisms.** In practice, this could include capital increases, hybrid capital instruments or sovereign guarantees to MDBs. By concentrating limited resources in institutions able to mobilise or intermediate larger volumes of finance, this option seeks to preserve the aggregate financial footprint of the multilateral development system and maintain delivery at scale. However, it also implies a shift in the composition of outflows towards non-concessional instruments, potentially reducing the share of grant-based and highly concessional support available to low-income and vulnerable countries, where needs are highest and access to alternative financing is most constrained.
2. **Preserve concessionality, even if total multilateral volumes decline as a result of reduced leverage.** Under this option, donors could protect grants and other concessional flows to ensure continued support for the poorest countries and those with limited access to alternative financing. While this approach safeguards support to contexts where multilateral development finance plays a critical stabilising role, it comes at the cost of a smaller overall footprint and a reduced capacity to finance large-scale investments.
3. **Apply proportional cuts across institutions and instruments (often described as a "haircut" approach).** This strategy spreads reductions evenly and may be perceived as politically simpler or more neutral, as it avoids explicit prioritisation of activities or institutions. However, it is the least strategic response to constrained budgets. Because it applies cuts indiscriminately between institutions, mandates, contexts and instruments rather than concentrating resources where they can generate the greatest impact, it risks eroding the comparative advantages of several parts of the multilateral development system and thus weakening the system's ability to deliver. Rather than preserving balance, across-the-board cuts can dilute impact by forcing all organisations to retrench simultaneously, regardless of their role, leverage capacity or relevance to the poorest and most vulnerable contexts.

These three scenarios illustrate why the frequently invoked ambition for the multilateral development system to "do more with less" is unrealistic. When overall envelopes shrink, the system cannot simultaneously preserve volumes *and* concessionality. Reduced resources inevitably translate into trade-offs between scale and support to the poorest and most vulnerable contexts. The question facing donors is therefore not whether the system can absorb cuts without consequences, but which consequences they are willing to accept. In this sense, declining multilateral contributions require not doing more with less, but doing differently through deliberate, strategic choices about what to protect, what to scale back and how to align scarce resources with collective priorities.

Figure 3.13. Donor choices on how to allocate multilateral contributions involve explicit trade-offs

Illustrative trade-offs of aid funding cuts: 15% budget cuts scenario

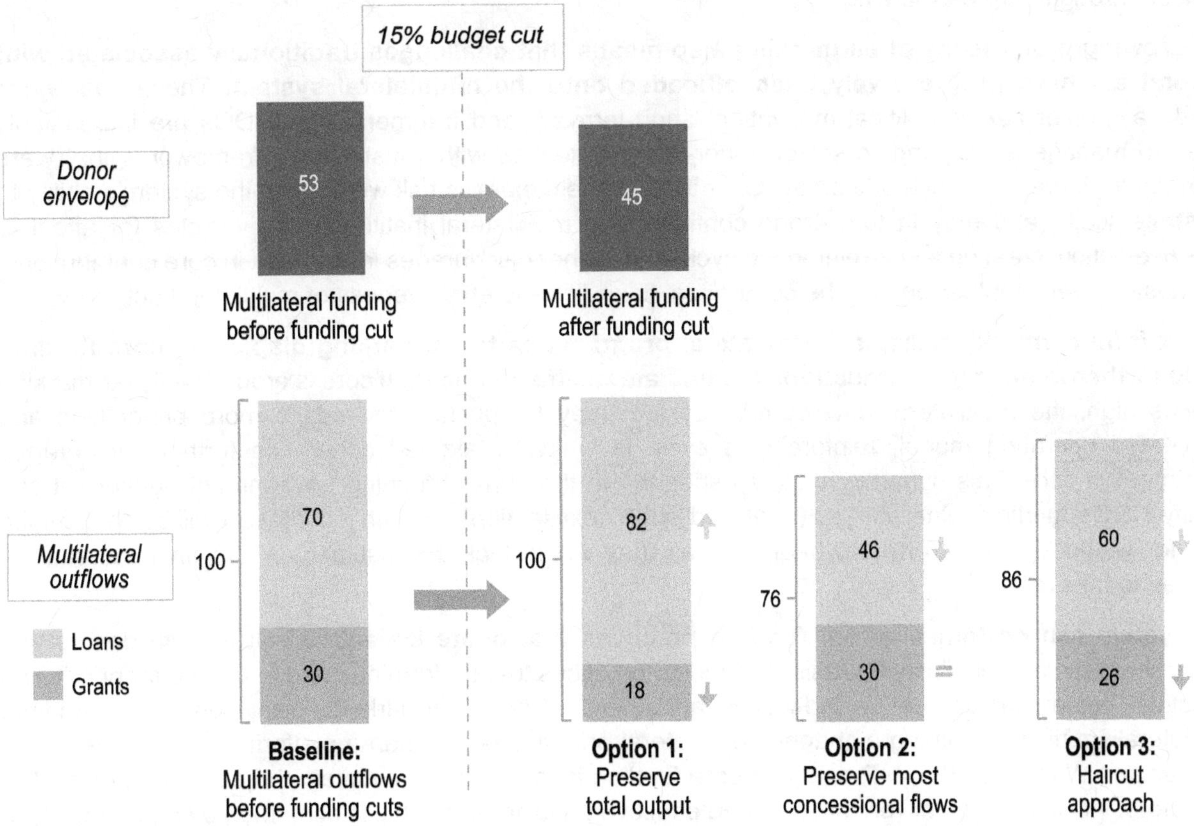

Note: To keep the illustration transparent, the simulation assumes simplified leverage relationships: grant financing is treated as having a one-to-one relationship between donor cost and financing delivered, while loans are assumed to generate three dollars of financing for each dollar of donor contribution. The baseline scenario assumes an outflow composition of 30% grants and 70% loans, broadly representative of the historical balance between concessional and non-concessional multilateral finance.

3.2.2. The growing use of earmarked funding risks compounding the effects of declining multilateral contribution and threatens the foundations of multilateral effectiveness

In a context of constrained budgets, pressures to preserve visibility, attribution and control increasingly influence donors' choices between core and earmarked funding, as discussed in Section 3.1.3. These modality choices matter because they affect not only what the multilateral development system delivers, but also its capacity to plan, co-ordinate and sustain collective action over time. This section examines how the changing role of earmarked funding has implications that go beyond headline funding volumes.

The trend towards greater earmarking points to a continued "bilateralisation" of multilateral development finance, whereby donors increasingly use earmarked contributions to pursue national priorities through multilateral channels. While earmarked funding can expand the volume of resources available to international organisations, enabling higher levels of activity in the short term (Heinzel, Reinsberg and Zaccaria, 2024[15]), at the same time, evidence shows that growing reliance on earmarked funding can fragment financing, increase administrative burdens, and constrain multilateral organisations' flexibility in allocating resources in line with collectively agreed priorities (Ihl et al., 2025[16]). Moreover, core contributions remain structurally essential for multilateral organisations to deliver on their mandates. Being predictable and unearmarked, they underpin strategic planning, support governance and oversight functions, and allow institutions to allocate resources in line with their own agreed priorities rather than donor-specific preferences (OECD, 2024[6]). Core funding also enables multilateral organisations to invest in cross-cutting capabilities, co-ordination and long-term programming that cannot be efficiently financed through hard earmarking.

The growing prominence of earmarking also means that challenges traditionally associated with bilateral aid have progressively been offloaded onto the multilateral system. These challenges include a greater risk of political motivation, short-termism and fragmentation. MDOs are increasingly asked to manage an expanding set of donor-driven priorities within institutional frameworks that were designed to deliver collective outcomes. Over time, these dynamics risk weakening the system's ability to act strategically, and may in turn erode confidence in multilateral institutions as vehicles for effective collective action, creating a self-reinforcing cycle that further discourages investment in core contributions. This has concrete implications for the coherence, flexibility and effectiveness of multilateral action.

A shift from earmarking displacing bilateral programmes to earmarking displacing core funding would further weaken the foundations of multilateral effectiveness. If core is eroded while earmarking remains high, the multilateral development system may be pushed towards a more projectised and fragmented operating model, reinforcing a cycle in which weakened coherence further discourages investment in core. This dynamic matters especially in the current funding environment because it can amplify MDOs' funding vulnerabilities (analysed in the next section). In such a context, it will be challenging even for well-designed reforms to bear fruit, as they would lack the institutional and financial stability required to take root.

The system can no longer afford funding practices that dilute collective value. Both donors and MDOs share the responsibility for resisting funding practices that undermine coherence and for prioritising collective value addition over individual attribution. When earmarking displaces core funding, multilateralism risks becoming a channel for bilateral priorities rather than a platform for collective action (Sridhar and Woods, 2013[17]). Preserving core funding is important to maintain the conditions that allow multilateral institutions to deliver coherent and effective programmes. This is confirmed by research which shows that high reliance on earmarked funding can distort organisational incentives and performance (Baumann, 2021[18]; Reinsberg, 2023[19]).

Under present conditions, it may be unrealistic in the short term to expect donors and MDOs to significantly reduce their reliance on earmarked funding. As shown in Section 3.2.3, earmarked contributions can, in specific circumstances, provide short-term relief when organisations face abrupt defunding. However, while earmarking may offer tactical flexibility in the short run, the medium- to long-term objective should be to prevent it from structurally displacing core resources, or at least to encourage the use of broader thematic earmarking rather than tightly specified project-level restrictions (OECD, 2020[20]).

A more practical approach in the short term could therefore be to ensure that earmarked funding reinforces rather than undermines institutional mandates. In practice, this could mean assessing whether earmarked funding reflects a "triple alignment" between donors' national interests, collectively agreed multilateral priorities and partner countries' development strategies. When this alignment is in place, earmarked funding can complement core resources and enhance responsiveness without fragmenting the system. When it is absent, earmarking risks accelerating the drift towards bilateralisation and weakening the foundations of multilateral effectiveness (Schmid, Reitzenstein and Hall, 2021[21]).

Operationalising this approach may require donors to clearly articulate in their multilateral engagement strategies and operational processes how and for what purposes they intend to use different funding modalities. Evidence from donor good practice shows that making such strategies explicit and public enhances transparency for multilateral partners and partner countries, clarifying the intended role of modalities such as earmarking within an overall engagement framework (OECD, 2021[22]). It also strengthens internal coherence within donor administrations by guiding staff on when and how earmarked contributions are justified. At the operational level, embedding the "triple alignment" principle into internal processes could help ensure that earmarked funding decisions are consistent with both collective priorities and institutional mandates.

3.2.3. Funding vulnerability differs markedly across multilateral development organisations

While changes in funding volumes and modalities have systemic implications for the scale, focus and effectiveness of multilateral development finance, how they affect individual organisations varies. The same aggregate funding choices can translate into very different pressures for individual multilateral development organisations depending on their funding models, donor concentration and diversification, and their institutional capacity to swiftly adapt to changing funding environments (Eijking, 2026[23]). As a result, constrained funding does not affect the system evenly but instead creates differentiated vulnerabilities that can reinforce existing structural imbalances. This section shifts the focus from system-wide implications to organisation-level exposure, examining which parts of the multilateral development system are most at risk in the current funding environment and how they can mitigate this exposure.

Different funding structures translate similar donor cuts into very different institutional risks

How MDOs are affected by donor cuts depends as much on the size of the reduction as on the organisation's key dimensions of vulnerability. These include whether the organisation's funding model is grant-based versus leveraged, the concentration of its donor base, the balance between funding modalities, and the extent to which it can draw on private sources of finance (Table 3.1). Depending on these dimensions, the same reduction in donor contributions can translate into very different operational impacts from one institution to another. Table 3.1 summarises how these vulnerability dimensions shape the way funding cuts are transmitted through the system. Rather than representing isolated risks, the dimensions often interact, amplifying exposure for individual organisations.

Table 3.1. Key vulnerability dimensions determine how a multilateral development organisation will be affected by funding cuts

Key vulnerability dimension	Primary exposure	Implications	Examples
Predominantly grant-based funding model	Direct pass-through of donor cuts	Immediate pressure on programmes and staffing in case of funding cuts	Most UNDS entities and vertical funds
High donor concentration	Dependence on decisions of a small number of major contributors	Abrupt adjustments following individual donor allocation decisions	IOM, UNHCR, WFP
High reliance on voluntary or earmarked contributions	Exposure to shifts in short-term political priorities, including crisis reallocations (e.g. security, migration)	Reduced predictability and constrained medium-term planning in cases where funding is short-term or tightly earmarked. The activities and mandates of organisations are driven and determined by a limited number of funders' strategic priorities with a narrow view of results that may neglect corporate functions or normative work.	UNAIDS, UNICEF, WFP
Limited private funding	Exposure to correlated fiscal tightening among public donors	Limited resource diversification to buffer and absorb system-wide funding fluctuations, particularly when multiple public donors adjust budgets simultaneously.	FAO, UNIDO, WIPO

Funding models are a primary determinant of resilience, with grant-based organisations structurally more exposed to funding contractions than leveraged institutions. Grant-funded MDOs, such as most UNDS entities, rely directly on sustained donor inflows to maintain operations. By contrast, MDBs can absorb short to medium-term funding shocks more effectively by leveraging their balance sheets and capital markets access. Vertical funds occupy an intermediate position: while multi-year replenishments provide short to medium-term predictability, narrow donor bases can leave them highly exposed when replenishment cycles coincide with periods of fiscal tightening or shifting donor priorities. This is illustrated by the dynamics of the latest Global Fund's recent replenishment: at the November 2025 Global Fund Summit, four of the seven top contributors to the fund, which collectively provide around 90% of total pledged funding, announced lower pledges than in the previous cycle, while the other three were not ready to pledge (Madan Keller, Bonnifield and Baker, 2026[24]).

Where organisations are dependent on just a few donors for funding, this can amplify exposure to donor shifts and increase the likelihood of abrupt adjustments. Changes in the fiscal position, political priorities or strategic orientation of a single donor can have disproportionate effects. In such cases, even modest reductions in funding may trigger rapid adjustments in staffing, programme scope and thematic or geographic coverage. Overall, organisations with broader, more balanced and diversified donor bases are better positioned to smooth shocks over time and reallocate resources internally, reducing the need for sudden scaling back of their operations.

The scale and concentration of funding cuts among traditional donors highlight the need to rethink burden-sharing – not only between traditional and emerging donors, but also within the DAC itself. While Section 3.1.4 emphasised the importance of engaging non-DAC and emerging contributors, recent trends also reveal the imbalances among DAC members in supporting systemically important MDOs. UNHCR illustrates this vulnerability particularly clearly. In 2023, DAC members accounted for 98% of the organisation's government funding, and within that group, the United States alone represented 58% of DAC contributions. Such concentration leaves the UN's leading refugee actor structurally exposed to domestic political cycles in a single member state. Cases of this kind point to the need for more deliberate burden-sharing among DAC members.

The balance between funding modalities also plays a central role in shaping MDOs' funding stability. Institutions that receive a significant share of core, assessed contributions (legally binding contributions based on agreed burden-sharing formulas) tend to benefit from greater funding predictability and short-term protection from funding vulnerability. Conversely, organisations that rely predominantly on voluntary funding are more exposed to fluctuations driven by donors' annual budget cycles, shifting priorities and crisis-driven reallocations. Where assessed funding is limited, and voluntary earmarked resources dominate, funding volatility from member states becomes a structural feature, often translating into constraints on medium-term planning. Yet, as the UNESCO case below illustrates, voluntary funding can, in specific and time-bound circumstances, help offset losses from individual donors in the short term, even if it does not necessarily provide a durable substitute for predictable core resources.

Access to private funding can partially mitigate exposure to public funding cycles but remains limited and uneven across the system. Contributions from private actors, philanthropic foundations and NGOs have the potential to buffer individual organisations from correlated fiscal tightening by government donors. However, reliance on a small number of large private contributors can also create new forms of concentration risk if their priorities shift. However, as shown in Section 3.1, such funding remains modest at the system level and highly concentrated in a small number of entities. As a result, private funding can strengthen resilience for some organisations but is insufficient to offset systemic shocks affecting public donors as a group.

Diversification opportunities also extend beyond bilateral and private sources. In some cases, multilateral development organisations receive significant resources from other multilateral actors such as vertical funds, which can provide an additional layer of funding diversification. For example, in 2025 the

United Nations Environment Programme (UNEP) received almost half of its funding (48%) from the Global Environment Facility (GEF) and the Green Climate Fund (GCF) (UNEP, 2026[25]). Such arrangements can partially reduce exposure to fluctuations in bilateral donors' budgets. However, vertical funds themselves rely on periodic replenishments and relatively concentrated donor bases, meaning that they are not immune to broader fiscal tightening. While they can strengthen resilience at the level of individual organisations, they do not eliminate systemic vulnerability.

Across the UNDS, multiple dimensions of vulnerability often coincide, creating particularly high exposure to funding contractions. Figure 3.14 maps UNDS entities across three dimensions: reliance on voluntary (i.e. non-assessed) funding, concentration of the government donor base, and the share of private funding (i.e. private sector, philanthropic foundations and NGOs in this case). A defining characteristic of UNDS entities' funding mix is the systemic dependence on voluntary funding, with the majority of agencies relying on voluntary contributions for at least 90% of their total resources. Organisations combining high donor concentration, heavy reliance on voluntary funding and limited access to private resources (such as IOM, WFP, UNAIDS and UNODC) emerge as particularly exposed to reductions in multilateral contributions. Only 4 of the 25 UNDS entities featured in Figure 3.14 attract more than 10% of their funding from private sources (UNICEF, WHO, UNHCR and the International Telecommunication Union), suggesting that while it can provide some buffer at the level of individual entities, private funding remains insufficient to provide meaningful resilience to the system as a whole.

Figure 3.14. Most UNDS entities exhibit a high reliance on voluntary contributions

Share of voluntary funding (%), government donor concentration (0-100) and share of private funding of UNDS entities, 2023-2024 average

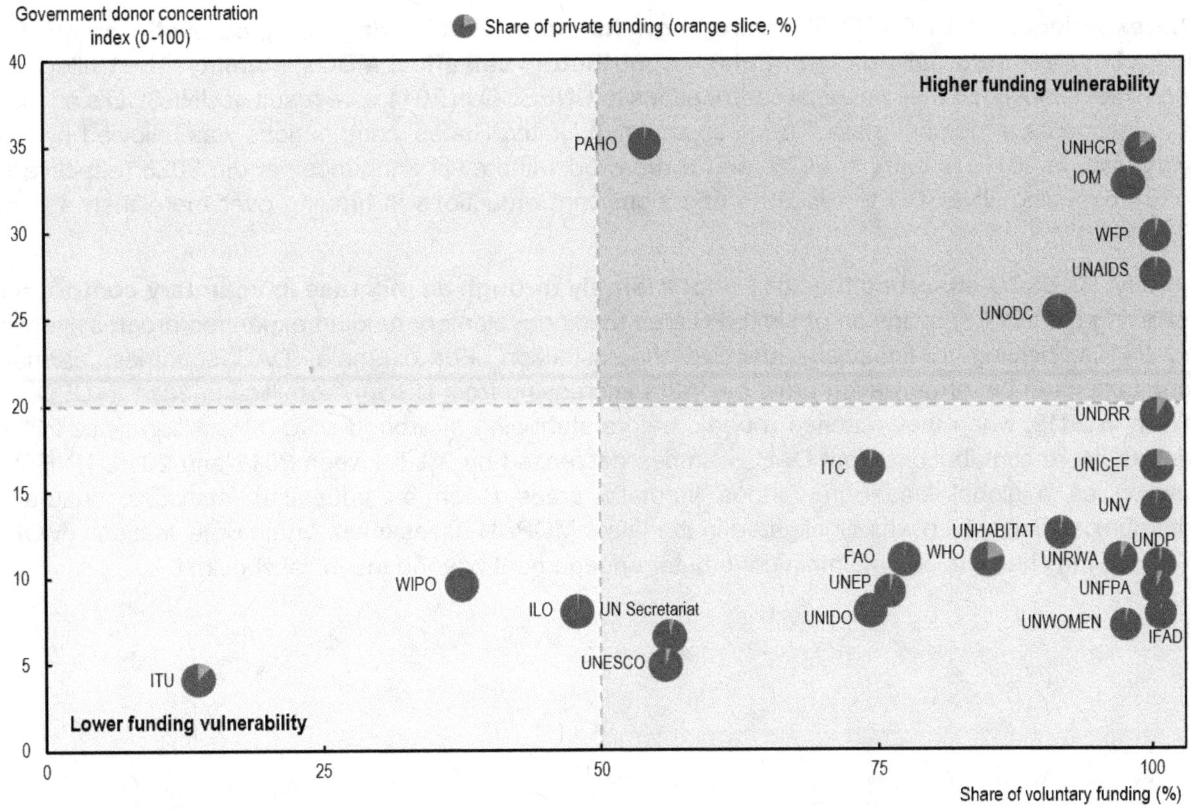

Note: The share of voluntary funding ranges from 0% (only assessed funding) to 100% (only voluntary funding). The government donor concentration index captures whether each organisation's funding from official bilateral donors is evenly distributed amongst all government donors (0) or whether it is concentrated amongst just a few (100). The share of private funding (%) represents the proportion of funding from the private sector, foundations and NGOs in total funding and is represented by the orange slice in each blue pie. The chart includes all entities in the UNDS except those with 10 or fewer government donors in both 2023 and 2024. The chart excludes local contributions (i.e. funding provided by a government to UN activities implemented in its own country) from analysis.
Source: Authors' calculations based on datasets of donor contributions to the United Nations Development System (UNDS) in 2023 and 2024 provided directly by United Nations Department of Economic and Social Affairs (UNDESA).

Funding vulnerability is closely linked to organisational mandates, implying that funding diversification strategies cannot be uniform across institutions. Agencies with significant humanitarian operations tend to attract a larger share of private and philanthropic funding, reflecting donor preferences for visible, time-bound and crisis-oriented interventions. This pattern is consistent with evidence showing that aid framed as humanitarian relief or disaster response attracts higher public support than aid framed around long-term development or institutional reform (Munnelly and Pfitzner, 2025[26]). Organisations without a strong humanitarian profile (such as UNDP or UNEP) face greater constraints in mobilising private funding and may need to be clearer about the value of their activities. Other organisations may be cautious about engaging with the private sector due to reputational risks, including concerns about undue influence. The recent emphasis placed by UNDP's leadership on expanding private fundraising illustrates growing recognition of both the opportunities and challenges of diversification (Hancock and Dubois, 2026[27]). UNESCO offers an example of how organisations can mitigate funding vulnerability – in its case, following several withdrawals by a major donor.

The case of UNESCO illustrates both the opportunities and limits of MDOs' response to funding shocks

The experience of UNESCO illustrates how funding volatility driven by domestic political and budget cycles in a small number of major contributors can affect MDOs' stability. The United States and Israel suspended their financial contributions to UNESCO in 2011 as a result of UNESCO's admission of Palestine as a member state. The suspension in United States' contributions was followed by formal withdrawal in 2017, re-entry in 2023, and a renewed withdrawal announcement in 2025 (effective end-2026), exposing UNESCO to repeated and significant reductions in funding over more than a decade (Figure 3.15).

Initially, UNESCO absorbed the 2011 shock largely through an increase in voluntary contributions. Following the 2011 suspension of United States funding, voluntary funding expanded progressively over the 2010s, helping to financially stabilise the institution. For example, DAC countries' earmarked contributions to the organisation grew by 162%, increasing from USD 47.2 million in 2011 to USD 123.5 million in 2019, when they reached a peak, before stabilising at around USD 115 million since 2021. In contrast, core contributions from DAC countries decreased by 9% between 2011 and 2019. UNESCO's position as a global leader in various thematic areas (such as education, statistics, culture and communications), which was highlighted in the latest MOPAN assessment of the organisations (MOPAN, 2025[28]), may have helped maintain contributor engagement beyond the initial shock.

Figure 3.15. The composition of DAC countries' funding to UNESCO has shifted in recent years

DAC countries' core and earmarked contributions to UNESCO, 2011-2024, and US funding decisions

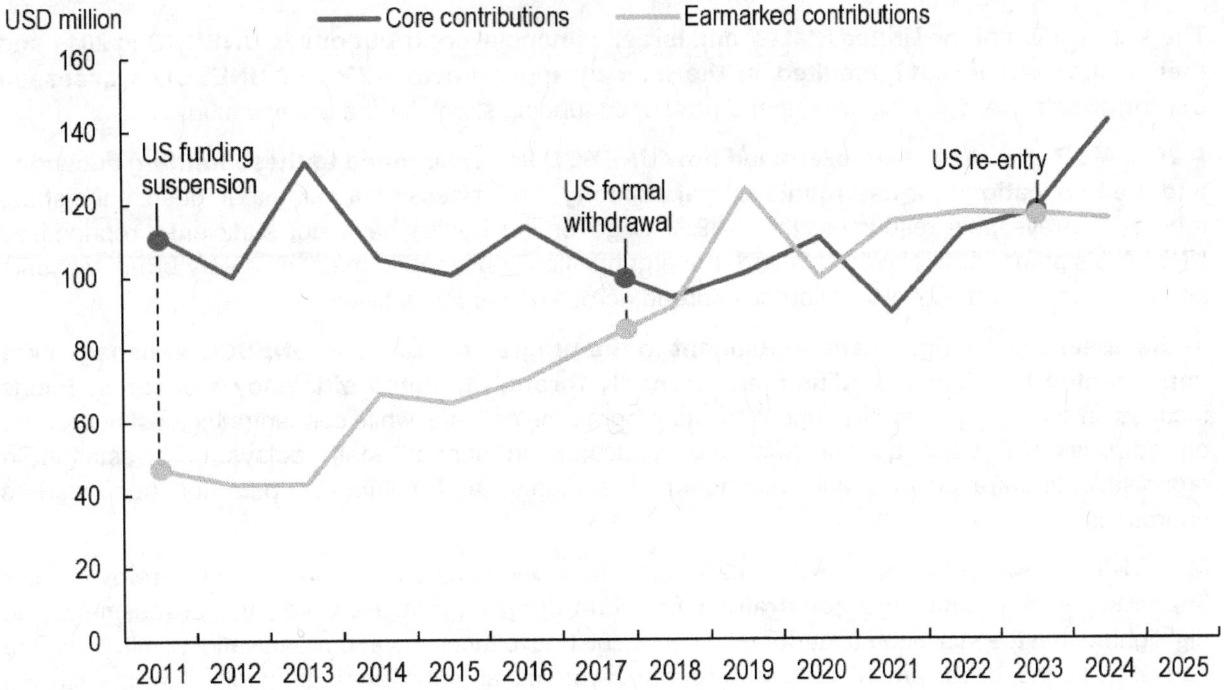

Note: Calculations are based on disbursements, in 2023 constant prices. Data used in this graph is based on DAC countries' reporting to the OECD Creditor Reporting System (CRS).
Source: Authors' calculations based on OECD (2026[2]), Providers' Total Use of the Multilateral System (dataset), http://data-explorer.oecd.org/s/1td.

Beyond these short-term adjustments, UNESCO is pursuing various longer-term adaptation strategies. These include efforts to further diversify its donor base, adjust expenditures, and continue reforms already underway, including ensuring the alignment of voluntary contributions with the organisation's core mandates, in accordance with UNESCO's strategy. Although the organisation has also engaged in risk anticipation and mitigation, the most recent withdrawal by the United States is still expected to have material financial and operational effects.

Recent evidence provides a more detailed picture of the implications of the organisation's funding volatility over the past decade. The 2020 and 2025 MOPAN assessments of UNESCO have examined how the organisation managed and was impacted by the successive funding suspensions and withdrawals (Box 3.2).

Box 3.2. MOPAN's assessments of UNESCO underscore that limited reprioritisation in the face of funding shocks can constrain organisational effectiveness

The suspension of the United States' and Israel's financial contributions to UNESCO in 2011 and their withdrawal in 2017 resulted in the loss of approximately 22% of UNESCO's assessed contributions, creating a significant and prolonged funding shock for the organisation.

A 2020 MOPAN assessment examined how UNESCO had responded to these funding decisions and the implications for its organisational capacity. The assessment found that, despite the sharp reduction in available resources, the UNESCO governing bodies have not sufficiently reprioritised UNESCO's programme of work. Instead, the organisation continued to maintain a very broad mandate and programme portfolio, with resources spread across numerous activities.

In the absence of a significant adjustment to the programme of work, UNESCO's management implemented the financial adjustment primarily through targeted efficiency measures. Efforts focused on protecting normative functions and programme delivery, while concentrating cost reductions on administrative capacity. This included reductions in support staff, delays in investment in organisational infrastructure and management systems, and tighter budgets for headquarters operations.

MOPAN's follow-up assessment in 2025 found that UNESCO continued to deliver relevant and impactful work despite the constrained financial environment. However, the assessment also highlighted that the sustained underfunding of administrative functions and organisational infrastructure had slowed the development of key corporate systems and management tools, thereby limiting UNESCO's overall organisational effectiveness, even against a backdrop of generally satisfactory organisational performance.

The decision by the United States to rejoin UNESCO in 2023 therefore represented a critical opportunity to reinforce key functions that had remained under-resourced, including the field office network. While the organisation took a prudent approach to allocating these additional funds, the renewed withdrawal of the United States reopens the question of how to resource key functions in a sustainable manner. Uncertainty regarding the payment of the 2025 contribution nevertheless adds further short-term financial pressure.

Source: MOPAN (2025[28]) *MOPAN Assessment Report: United Nations Educational, Scientific and Cultural Organization (UNESCO) (Part I)*, https://www.mopan.org/en/our-work/performance-evidence/unesco.html; and MOPAN (2019[29]) *United Nations Educational, Scientific and Cultural Organization (UNESCO) 2017-18 Performance Assessment*, https://www.mopan.org/content/dam/mopan/en/publications/our-work/evidence/unesco/unesco-2019/mopan-unesco-assessment-report-2019.pdf.

The UNESCO case highlights both the possibilities and the limits of organisational adaptation to funding volatility. Overall, the case highlights the dual role of voluntary funding: while excessive reliance on it increases vulnerability and undermines predictability, it can, under specific conditions, provide short-term relief to cushion abrupt funding shocks. However, such temporary increases in voluntary funding cannot substitute for aligning mandates, programmes and resources over time. As emphasised in the latest MOPAN assessment of UNESCO, stricter mandate discipline and prioritisation by governing bodies are also necessary to strengthen resilience and ensure that constrained resources are used effectively (MOPAN, 2025[28]). In response to this, UNESCO is currently considering a reform package 'UNESCO80 Roadmap' dealing with, inter alia, the financial aspects as well as the mandate focus.

References

African Center for Economic Transformation (2025), *Historic African Development Fund replenishment signals a new era for African-led development*, African Center for Economic Transformation, https://acetforafrica.org/research-and-analysis/insights-ideas/articles/historic-african-development-fund-replenishment-signals-a-new-era-for-african-led-development/#:~:text=The%20pledging%20session%20for%20the,over%20ADF%2D16%27s%20%248.9%20billion. [10]

African Development Fund (2025), *ADF-17 Replenishment: In historic move, African countries race to contribute to continent's development*, https://adf.afdb.org/adf-17-replenishment-in-historic-move-african-countries-race-to-contribute-to-continents-development/. [11]

Baumann, M. (2021), "How earmarking has become self-perpetuating in United Nations development co-operation", *Development Policy review*, Vol. 39/3, pp. 343-359, https://doi.org/10.1111/dpr.12504. [18]

Dag Hammarskjöld Foundation; UN MPTFO (2017), *Financing the UN Development System: Pathways to Reposition for Agenda 2030*, https://www.daghammarskjold.se/wp-content/uploads/2017/08/Financial-Instr-Report-2017_interactive.pdf. [5]

Eijking, J. (2026), "Time frames: Crisis expertise and rapid response mechanisms", *Review of International Studies*, Vol. First View, pp. 1-17, https://doi.org/10.1017/S0260210526101727. [23]

Hancock, A. and L. Dubois (2026), "UN seeks private finance drive for development projects", *Financial Times*, https://www.ft.com/content/0979b14c-5e9c-45ab-864f-b560c5fdf6c8. [27]

Heinzel, M., B. Reinsberg and G. Zaccaria (2024), "Core funding and the performance of international organizations: Evidence from UNDP projects", *Regulation & Governance*, Vol. 19/3, https://doi.org/10.1111/rego.12632. [15]

Ihl, J. et al. (2025), "The effectiveness of core and earmarked funding in multilateral development cooperation: Systematic review", *DEval Discussion Paper*, Vol. 02/2025, https://www.deval.org/fileadmin/Redaktion/PDF/05-Publikationen/Berichte/2025_Multilaterale_EZ/DEval-DP-02-2025-MultilateralDC-Web.pdf. [16]

Madan Keller, J., R. Bonnifield and P. Baker (2026), *A Radically Simplified Global Fund to Meet the Moment*, Center for Global Development, https://www.cgdev.org/publication/radically-simplified-global-fund-meet-moment. [24]

Martinez, N. and J. Estes (2025), *The ABCs of the IFIs: IDA21 Update*, Center for Global Development, https://www.cgdev.org/publication/abcs-ifis. [9]

Martinez, N. and C. Landers (2025), "Can IDA weather the development finance storm?", *Center for Global Development blog*, https://www.cgdev.org/blog/can-ida-weather-development-finance-storm. [8]

MOPAN (2025), *Mapping of Multilateral Organisations' Response to the Current Funding Environment*, Multilateral Organisation Performance Assessment Network, Paris, https://www.mopan.org/en/our-work/performance-insights/multilateral-effectiveness-in-a-shifting-landscape/mapping-thematic-brief.html. [3]

MOPAN (2025), *MOPAN Assessment Report: United Nations Educational, Scientific and Cultural Organization (UNESCO) (Part I)*, Multilateral Organisation Performance Assessment Network, Paris, https://www.mopan.org/en/our-work/performance-evidence/unesco.html. [28]

MOPAN (2019), *United Nations Educational, Scientific and Cultural Organization (UNESCO): 2017-18 Performance Assessment*, Multilateral Organisation Performance Assessment Network, Paris, https://www.mopan.org/content/dam/mopan/en/publications/our-work/evidence/unesco/unesco-2019/mopan-unesco-assessment-report-2019.pdf. [29]

Munnelly, C. and S. Pfitzner (2025), *Remaking the Case for International Development: Findings from a cross-country public opinion project*, Public First, https://www.publicfirst.co.uk/wp-content/uploads/2026/01/CIFF-v06sm.pdf. [26]

OECD (2026), *DAC1: Flows by provider (ODA+OOF+Private) (dataset)*, http://data-explorer.oecd.org/s/9w. [4]

OECD (2026), *Providers' Total Use of the Multilateral System (dataset)*, http://data-explorer.oecd.org/s/1td (accessed on 22 February 2026). [2]

OECD (2025), "Cuts in official development assistance: OECD projections for 2025 and the near term", *OECD Policy Briefs*, No. 26, OECD Publishing, Paris, https://doi.org/10.1787/8c530629-en. [1]

OECD (2024), *Multilateral Development Finance 2024*, OECD Publishing, Paris, https://doi.org/10.1787/8f1e2b9b-en. [6]

OECD (2021), *Partnering with the Multilateral System*, https://www.oecd.org/content/dam/oecd/en/publications/reports/2021/03/development-co-operation-tips-tools-insights-practices_d307b396/partnering-with-the-multilateral-system_72629d0f/ebed4316-en.pdf. [22]

OECD (2020), *Earmarked Funding to Multilateral Organisations: How is it used and what constitutes good practice?*, https://www.oecd.org/content/dam/oecd/en/publications/reports/2020/10/earmarked-funding-to-multilateral-organisations_bd41e2bd/a5620480-en.pdf. [20]

Reinsberg, B. (2023), "Earmarked funding and the performance of international organizations: Evidence from Food and Agricultural Development Agencies", *Global Studies Quarterly*, Vol. 3/4, https://doi.org/10.1093/isagsq/ksad056. [19]

Rigby, J. (2025), *Global vaccine group Gavi has $9 billion, short of its target*, https://www.reuters.com/business/healthcare-pharmaceuticals/global-vaccine-group-gavi-secures-9-billion-after-funding-summit-2025-06-25/#:~:text=The%20United%20Kingdom%20was%20the,in%20cutting%20international%20aid%20budgets. [12]

Schmid, L., A. Reitzenstein and N. Hall (2021), "Blessing or curse?: The effects of earmarked funding in UNICEF and UNDP", *Global Governance: A Review of Multilateralism and International Organizations*, Vol. 27/3, pp. 433-459, https://doi.org/10.1163/19426720-02703002. [21]

Sridhar and N. Woods (2013), "Trojan multilateralism: Global cooperation in health", *Global Policy*, Vol. 4/4, pp. 325-335, https://doi.org/10.1111/1758-5899.12066. [17]

UNEP (2026), *Our Planet. Our Purpose: UNEP Annual Report 2025*, United Nations Environment Programme, Nairobi, https://wedocs.unep.org/items/7f7ba2ae-c408-461e-91e7-b72146917ec6. [25]

UNESCO (2018), *UNESCO Executive appointments*, https://www.unesco.org/en/articles/unesco-executive-appointments. [7]

World Health Organization (2026), *Contributors (dataset)*, https://open.who.int/2024-25/contributors/contributor. [13]

World Health Organization (2025), *Audited Financial Statements for the Year Ended 31 December 2024*, World Health Organization, Geneva, https://apps.who.int/gb/ebwha/pdf_files/WHA78/A78_18-en.pdf. [14]

4 Financing from the multilateral development system

This chapter analyses outflows from the multilateral development system and assesses how recent trends and projected funding pressures are impacting its delivery capacity. It shows that while multilateral outflows reached a record high in 2024, this resilience masks mounting vulnerabilities. The expansion has been driven primarily by leveraged institutions, notably multilateral development banks, while grant-based entities are already experiencing contraction, particularly in humanitarian and social sectors. The chapter highlights emerging shifts in the geographic, sectoral and income distribution of multilateral finance. Looking ahead, it warns that without concrete action from multilateral stakeholders, several factors risk undermining the system's countercyclical role and its ability to support the poorest and most vulnerable.

4.1. Continued overall growth in multilateral outflows contrasts with early signs of strain in parts of the system

4.1.1. Multilateral outflows reached a new record high in 2024, but pressure is mounting beneath the surface

Total multilateral outflows reached a new peak in 2024, in part driven by MDBs' increasing lending capacity. As shown in Figure 4.1, multilateral outflows – which include both outflows from MDOs' core resources and earmarked flows channelled through them – totalled USD 296 billion in 2024, up 37% from pre-pandemic levels (2019) and 4% from 2023. This expansion reflects, in particular, the sustained increase in lending capacity among MDBs over the past decade, supported by periodic capital increases and successive reforms to their financial models.

The growing scale of multilateral outflows enables the system to play a crucial role in the broader development co-operation landscape. In recent decades, it has allowed MDOs to help address a growing number of global development challenges and crises and to play an important countercyclical role by expanding support to low and middle-income countries during major shocks. Previous editions of this report have documented how MDOs have repeatedly reoriented portfolios to respond to successive crises (OECD, 2022[1]; OECD, 2024[2]). This pattern is also visible in Figure 4.1: outflows rose sharply after the 2008 global financial crisis (from USD 109 billion in 2008 to USD 162 billion in 2009), and again at the onset of the 2020 COVID-19 crisis (from USD 216 billion in 2019 to USD 287 billion in 2020), highlighting the system's role as a stabilising force, even while global financing conditions are deteriorating.

Figure 4.1. Multilateral outflows have increased markedly over the past two decades in response to global crises

Evolution of multilateral outflows and their composition, 2004-2024

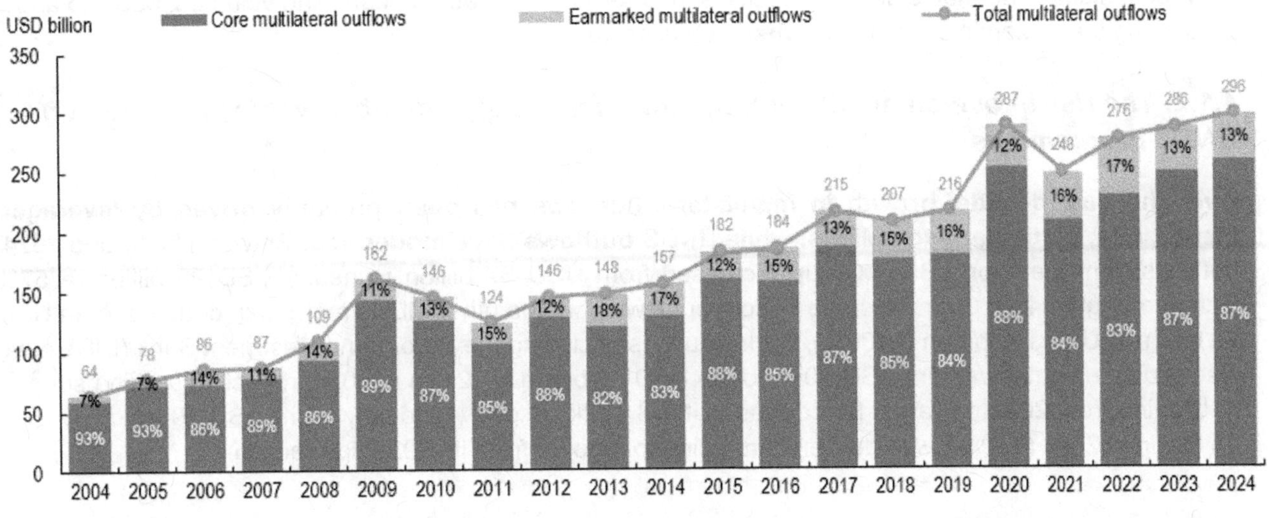

Note: Calculations are based on commitments, in 2023 constant prices. Calculations include ODA loans, ODA grants, OOF (excluding export credits), equity investments, and private sector instruments (PSIs).
Source: Authors' calculations based on OECD (2026[3]), *Creditor Reporting System* (dataset), https://data-explorer.oecd.org/s/52.

The composition of multilateral outflows helps explain both the system's scale and its resilience. In 2024, outflows financed from MDOs' core resources reached USD 258 billion (accounting for 87% of total multilateral outflows), while earmarked outflows amounted to USD 39 billion (13% of total) (Figure 4.1). This split matters because core resources are what underpins the system's surge capacity: they can be pooled and, for leveraged institutions, expanded through capital markets access. Earmarked outflows, by contrast, largely pass through on a one-to-one basis and therefore cannot, on their own, sustain the same countercyclical role. Protecting predictable core contributions is therefore not only a question of institutional stability – it also directly allows the system to scale when shocks hit developing countries (Chapter 3).

However, the growth and resilience described above masks the pressure building beneath the surface. Because much of the system operates through multi-year funding arrangements (e.g. replenishments) and, in the case of MDBs, through balance sheet models that smooth short-term fluctuations in shareholder funding, there is a lag between declining inflows and multilateral outflow contractions. While these features can temporarily cushion delivery and delay visible funding cuts, they also risk obscuring the extent of the underlying strain on the multilateral development system and delaying necessary adjustments.

Early signals of this adjustment are already emerging in parts of the system. While the cushioning effects of past replenishments and available balance sheet headroom may temporarily support multilateral commitments, these margins are finite. Once the buffers are exhausted, multilateral institutions may need to scale back existing or new commitments, increasing the risk of a sharper downturn in multilateral outflows than current headline figures suggest. Early signals of this adjustment are already emerging in parts of the system: findings from the 2025 MOPAN survey show that a growing number of MDOs have received formal donor notices of reduced funding and are implementing cost-containment measures, with direct implications for delivery (MOPAN, 2025[4]), as discussed in Section 4.2.1.

These dynamics risk weakening the system's countercyclical capacity at a time of heightened global instability. Any erosion of countercyclicality would have significant implications, particularly for countries facing debt distress, climate vulnerability or macroeconomic instability, which may experience reduced access to timely and adequate multilateral support in the event of an external shock. Protecting the mechanisms that enable surge capacity is therefore not only about sustaining volumes, but also about preserving the system's ability to act when needs spike.

4.1.2. *The rise in overall multilateral outflows masks already observable pressures on UNDS programmes*

Over the past decade, growth in multilateral outflows has been primarily driven by leveraged institutions, particularly the MDBs, while UNDS outflows have moderated. Between 2014 and 2024, outflows from the World Bank Group increased from USD 57 billion to nearly USD 90 billion, a 57% increase (Figure 4.2). Over the same period, outflows from the other MDBs more than doubled, from USD 49 billion to USD 103 billion (+109%). EU Institutions, including the European Investment Bank (EIB), have also scaled up outflows from USD 20 billion to USD 45 billion (+125%) in 2024, reflecting surging support to Ukraine from 2022 onwards. By contrast, UNDS outflows grew modestly, from USD 19 billion to USD 28 billion in 2024 (+49%), with delivery struggling to recover from its 2023 contraction.

Figure 4.2. The rise in multilateral outflows is driven by MDBs and EU Institutions

Evolution of multilateral outflows by provider type, 2014-2024

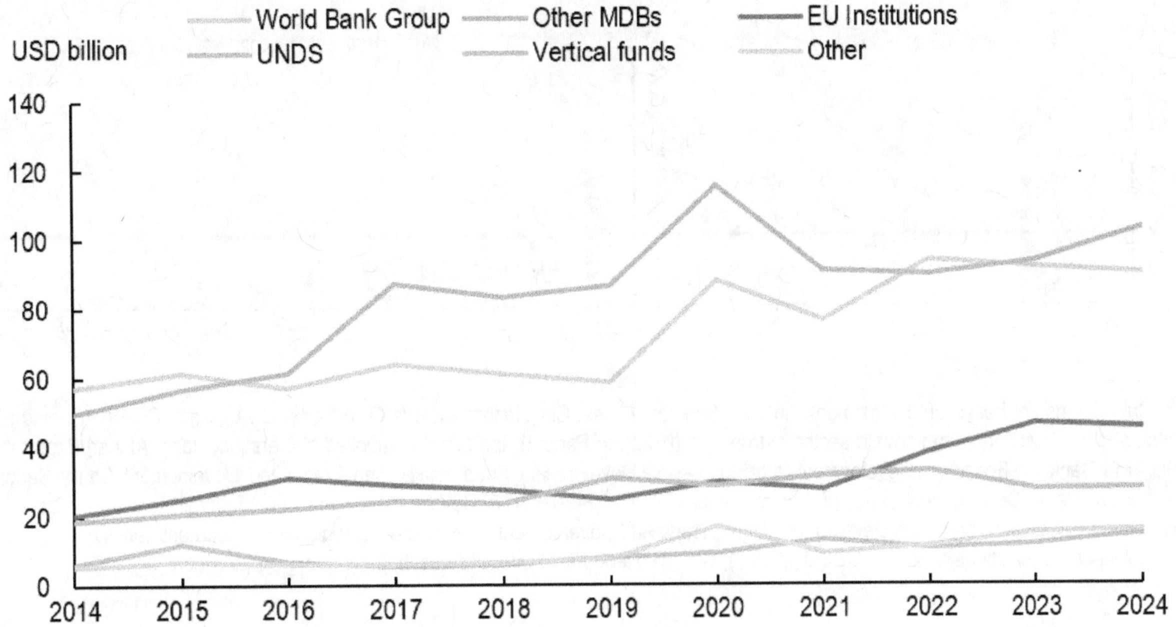

Note: Calculations are based on commitments, in 2023 constant prices. Calculations include ODA loans, ODA grants, OOF (excluding export credits), equity investment, and private sector instruments (PSI).
Source: Authors' calculations based on OECD (2026[3]), *Creditor Reporting System* (dataset), https://data-explorer.oecd.org/s/52.

This divergence between the outflows of leveraged institutions and those of the UNDS reflects structural differences in financing models and balance sheet capacity. MDBs have been able to scale and sustain higher levels of delivery due to capital increases, financial innovations and capital adequacy reforms implemented over the past decade. The introduction of the hybrid capital model under IDA18 in 2017, for example, reduced reliance on donor contributions and enabled IDA to diversify its funding base (OECD, 2022[1]). Similarly, the Asian Development Bank's consolidation of its concessional and ordinary capital resources significantly expanded its lending headroom (AsDB, 2025[5]). In 2024, AsDB outflows rose to USD 35 billion, up from USD 24 billion in 2023 and USD 19 billion in 2022 (Figure 4.3). More recently, financial innovations under the World Bank Group's evolution agenda have further increased capital efficiency. These reforms have translated directly into sustained lending capacity following recent global crises.

Figure 4.3. MDBs have continued to deliver increasing volumes of financing, driven by outflows from the World Bank Group and the AsDB

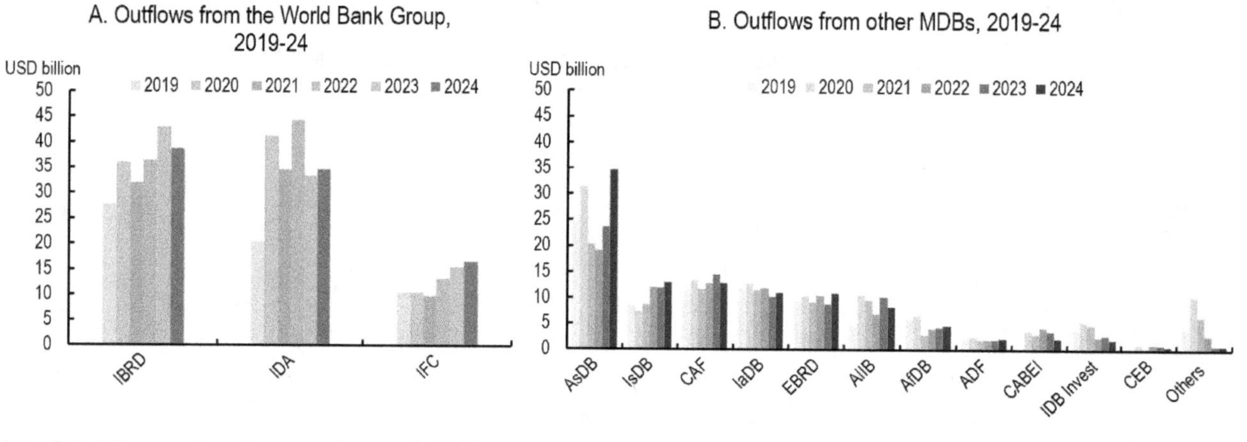

Note: Calculations are based on commitments, in 2023 constant prices. Calculations include ODA loans, ODA grants, OOF (excluding export credits), equity investments, and private sector instruments (PSIs). In Panel B, the last bar, labelled "Others", includes: African Export-Import Bank, Arab Bank for Economic Development in Africa, Asian Development Fund, Black Sea Trade and Development Bank, Caribbean Development Bank, Development Bank of Central African States, FONPLATA Development Bank, International Investment Bank, New Development Bank, North American Development Bank, Trade and Development Bank and other regional development banks.
Source: Authors' calculations based on OECD (2026[3]), *Creditor Reporting System* (dataset), https://data-explorer.oecd.org/s/52.

By contrast, grant-based institutions, such as UNDS entities, are less insulated from funding volatility and are already experiencing the effects of funding cuts on their delivery capacity. UNDS outflows declined 16% overall between 2022 and 2024: from USD 33 billion in 2022 to 27 billion in 2023, with a marginal recovery to 28 billion in 2024. Unlike leveraged institutions, which can temporarily absorb reductions in inflows through balance sheet mechanisms, grant-funded entities transmit funding shocks more directly into programme volumes. In the case of the UNDS' humanitarian entities, it is life-saving, hard-to-replace assistance to vulnerable groups which is at stake (Box 4.1).

The contraction is particularly pronounced among large humanitarian UNDS entities and is likely to persist in the medium term. Between 2022 and 2024, outflows from the WFP, the largest UNDS agency in volume of financing delivered, fell by nearly one third (-31%), declining from USD 8.2 billion to USD 5.6 billion (Figure 4.4) (Box 4.1). Over the same period, outflows from UNICEF declined by 14%, from USD 4.0 billion to USD 3.4 billion, while those from the UNHCR decreased by 21%, from USD 3.9 billion to USD 3.1 billion. Even steeper reductions were observed for UNDP and WHO, whose outflows fell by 48% and 42% respectively over the same period. These reductions reflect the high share of voluntary and earmarked funding in their financing structures, which limits their capacity to smooth shocks across programmes or regions to address short-term funding constraints (Dag Hammarskjöld Foundation, 2025[6]). Against the backdrop of the UN's ongoing liquidity constraints, continued pressure on financial resources may further constrain both the normative and operational activities of the UNDS, potentially affecting the scale, scope and predictability of its engagement across programme areas (Dag Hammarskjöld Foundation, 2025[6]).

Figure 4.4. Major UNDS organisations are already experiencing a significant drop in their outflows

Change in outflow volume among top UNDS organisations, 2022-2024

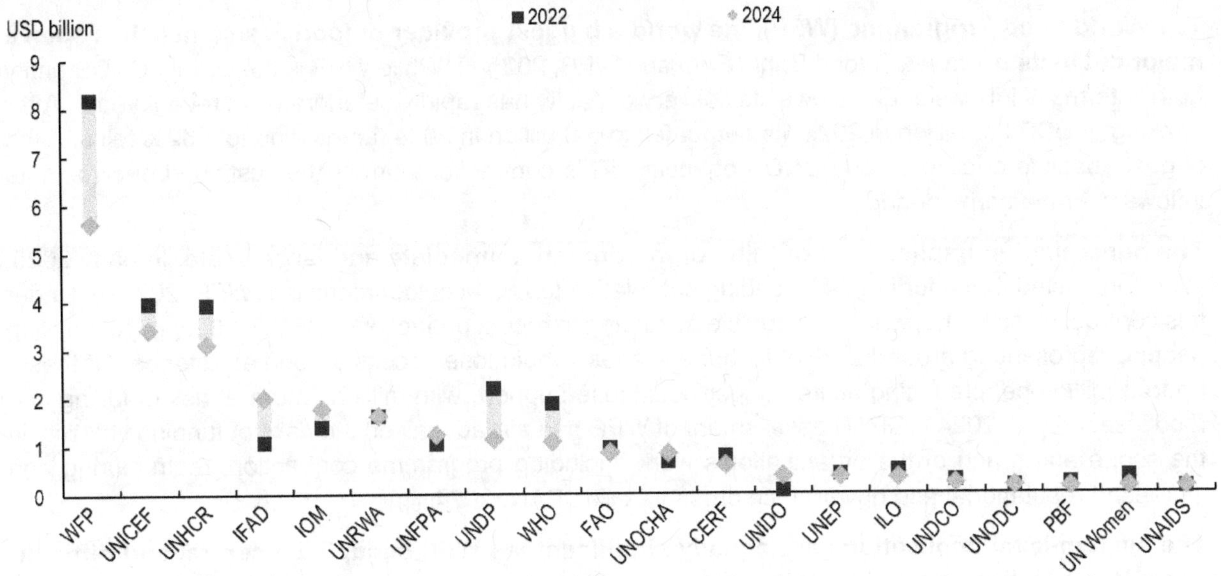

Note: Calculations are based on commitments, in 2023 constant prices.
Source: Authors' calculations based on OECD (2026[3]), *Creditor Reporting System* (dataset), https://data-explorer.oecd.org/s/52.

Contrasting outflow trends across the various MDO types signals that recent aggregate growth may mask asymmetries in individual MDOs' delivery capacity. While leveraged institutions continue to sustain or expand delivery, outflows from grant-based MDOs are already contracting, particularly in humanitarian and social sectors. As funding pressures intensify, these differences in financing models may increasingly shape not only who delivers more, but also where and to whom multilateral development finance flows. The story of the WFP is a case in point (Box 4.1).

Box 4.1. The case of the World Food Programme illustrates the direct implications of funding volatility for humanitarian aid

The World Food Programme (WFP), the world's biggest provider of food assistance, has seen a major cut in its outflows (World Bank, FAO and WFP, 2025[7]). While WFP is the largest UNDS entity both in terms of inflows and outflows, its delivery capacity has rapidly deteriorated in recent years. After peaking at USD 8.2 billion in 2022, its output fell to 5.6 billion in 2024, amounting to a 32% fall and the largest absolute decline among UNDS agencies. This contraction mirrors the sustained decline in its inflows over the same period.

The humanitarian implications of this contraction are immediate and large-scale. In early 2025, WFP forecasted that a further 34% funding cut relative to 2024 could materialise (WFP, 2025[8]). Under this contraction scenario, which is plausible according to recent projections (OECD, 2025[9]), 16.7 million people, representing around 21% of its beneficiaries, would lose access to food assistance. Of these, up to 3 million people facing acute hunger could lose support, with millions more at risk of falling into food insecurity. A 2024 MOPAN assessment of WFP had already raised the risks of funding volatility in the scope and reach of the organisation's work, including programme contraction, restructuring and increased reputational and governance pressures (MOPAN, 2024[10]).

The system-level implications are equally significant, as WFP occupies a central and difficult-to-replace position in highly fragile contexts. Eight of the eleven countries projected to experience the largest reductions in food assistance are active conflict settings where WFP has built operational presence over decades (WFP, 2025[8]). Previous editions of this report have shown that the ability to pursue operations in fragile and conflict-affected contexts is a comparative advantage of the multilateral development system (OECD, 2020[11]). In a context of widespread bilateral aid reductions, it is unlikely that any single actor could rapidly replicate WFP's reach, procurement systems or logistical networks.

The WFP case illustrates a broader systemic risk. When core grant-funded institutions contract, the loss in delivery is immediate, highly concentrated in vulnerable contexts, and difficult to offset. While leveraged institutions may cushion funding shocks temporarily, reductions affecting central humanitarian actors translate directly into diminished life-saving assistance. The majority of WFP's resources are earmarked and short-term, limiting flexibility in reallocating funds across operations or over time. As a result, funding volatility is transmitted almost one-to-one into programme contraction. This asymmetry reinforces the importance of considering distributional and delivery chain consequences when assessing funding reductions.

Source: World Bank, FAO and WFP (2025[7]), *Strengthening Strategic Grain Reserves to Enhance Food Security*, https://openknowledge.worldbank.org/server/api/core/bitstreams/9b5e0861-e981-4f9e-820a-84030ed1d981/content; WFP (2025[8]), *Food Security Impact of Reduction in WFP Funding*, https://docs.wfp.org/api/documents/WFP-0000166581/download/; OECD (2025[9]), "Cuts in official development assistance: OECD projections for 2025 and the near term", https://doi.org/10.1787/8c530629-en; MOPAN (2024[10]) *Performance at a Glance: World Food Programme (WFP)*, https://www.mopan.org/en/our-work/performance-evidence/wfp.html; OECD (2020[11]), *Multilateral Development Finance 2020*, https://doi.org/10.1787/e61fdf00-en.

4.1.3. *Recent crises have displaced the geographical and sectoral centre of gravity of multilateral development finance*

Multilateral outflows to Europe increased sharply after 2021, largely reflecting expanded support to Ukraine. Between 2021 and 2024, multilateral outflows to Europe more than tripled, rising from USD 17 billion to USD 51 billion (+201%) (Figure 4.5). Over the same period, outflows to Africa stagnated (-

1%), those to the Americas declined by 4% and those to the Middle East by 6%. Asia recorded a 26% increase and Oceania a 40% increase, though from a low base.

EU Institutions play a leading role in the support provided to Ukraine. In 2023-24, Ukraine accounted for nearly half (44% on average) of outflows from EU Institutions, compared with only 4% in 2021 (OECD, 2026[3]). While this surge highlights the European Union's capacity to mobilise significant resources in response to a major crisis at its borders, it also raises questions regarding the medium-term sustainability of such spending amid intensifying fiscal pressures across many EU member states.

Figure 4.5. Multilateral outflows to Europe have substantially increased in recent years, driven by support to Ukraine

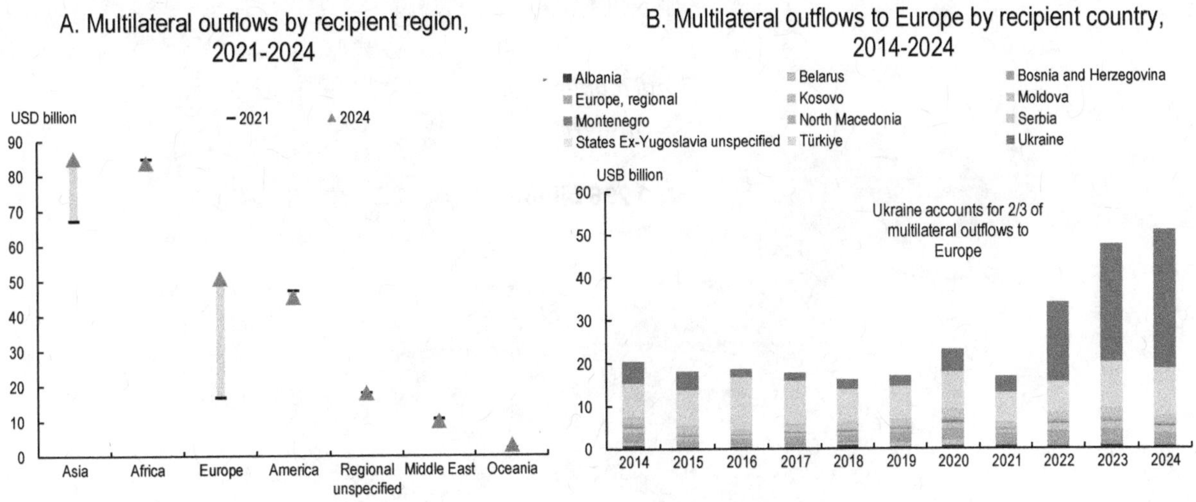

Note: Calculations are based on commitments, in 2023 constant prices. Calculations include ODA loans, ODA grants, OOF (excluding export credits), equity investments, and private sector instruments (PSIs).
Source: Authors' calculations based on OECD (2026[3]), *Creditor Reporting System* (dataset), https://data-explorer.oecd.org/s/52.

These geographic shifts reinforce a longer-term tilt of multilateral development finance towards middle-income countries. In 2024, three-quarters of multilateral outflows to developing countries were directed towards LMICs and UMICs. By contrast, LICs received only 10% of total multilateral outflows: USD 31 billion, of which Ethiopia alone accounted for USD 7 billion. Since 2014, outflows to UMICs have increased by 109% and to LMICs by 81%, compared to growth of 55% for LICs.

Multilateral outflows are also increasingly concentrated in a small number of countries. In 2024, Ukraine alone received more than one-tenth of total multilateral outflows to developing countries (11%), up from around 2% between 2014 and 2021 (Figure 4.6). This increase resulted in Ukraine receiving a larger volume of multilateral outflows in 2024 than the 25 LICs combined. More broadly, the top 20 recipient countries together accounted for more than half of total multilateral outflows. Such concentration may reflect legitimate crisis-response priorities and large-scale infrastructure operations in middle-income countries, but it also raises questions about the distributional effects of recent crises.

Figure 4.6. Middle-income countries receive three-quarters of multilateral outflows

Multilateral outflows received by developing countries by income group and recipient country, 2024, in USD billion

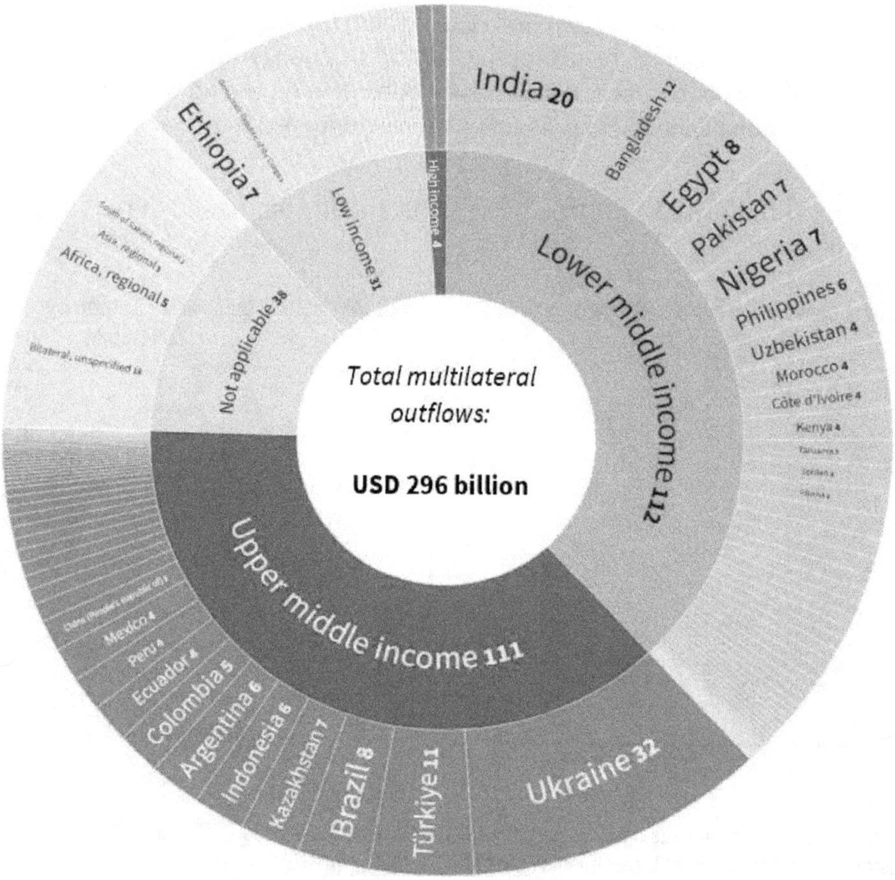

Note: Calculations are based on commitments, in 2023 constant prices. Calculations include ODA loans, ODA grants, OOF (excluding export credits), equity investment, and private sector instruments (PSIs). Recipient country income groups refer to the World Bank income group classification. The category "not applicable" corresponds primarily to activities that are regional or global in nature.
Source: Authors' calculations based on OECD (2026[3]), *Creditor Reporting System* (dataset), https://data-explorer.oecd.org/s/52. Calculations used the World Bank (2026[12]) 2024 country income group classification, https://datahelpdesk.worldbank.org/knowledgebase/articles/906519-world-bank-country-and-lending-groups. As Ethiopia was not classified in 2024, the World Bank (2024[13]) 2023 classification (low income) was applied, https://blogs.worldbank.org/en/opendata/world-bank-country-classifications-by-income-level-for-2024-2025.

Crisis response has also reshaped the sectoral composition of multilateral portfolios, with potential long-term consequences. The succession of major global crises in recent years has required multilateral organisations to reallocate resources towards immediate and emerging priorities. The COVID-19 pandemic prompted a temporary surge in social sector spending, as multilateral portfolios pivoted towards health, emergency response and social protection (OECD, 2024[2]). As shown in Figure 4.7, the share of multilateral outflows allocated to the social sector increased from 16% in 2019 to 23% in 2020 and further to 27% in 2021. As pandemic-related pressures eased, resources were redirected towards budget support for Ukraine, recorded under the governance category, underscoring the continued crisis-driven reorientation of multilateral portfolios.

While this reorientation has enabled crisis response, it has also narrowed the space for longer-term development investment. Infrastructure financing, for example, fell from 33% of total multilateral outflows in 2014 to around 21% over the period 2020-2023 (Figure 4.7). Although multilateral development finance has grown in volume over the past decade, current and expected funding constraints mean that continued prioritisation of short-term crisis response could increasingly crowd out long-term development. Given the central role of long-term development in driving countries' productivity growth, climate resilience and structural transformation, this shift may ultimately constrain long-term development trajectories, especially in countries that have little or no alternatives to public finance.

Figure 4.7. The distribution of multilateral outflows by sector reflects a shift towards short-term crisis response

Distribution of multilateral outflows by macro sector, 2014-2024

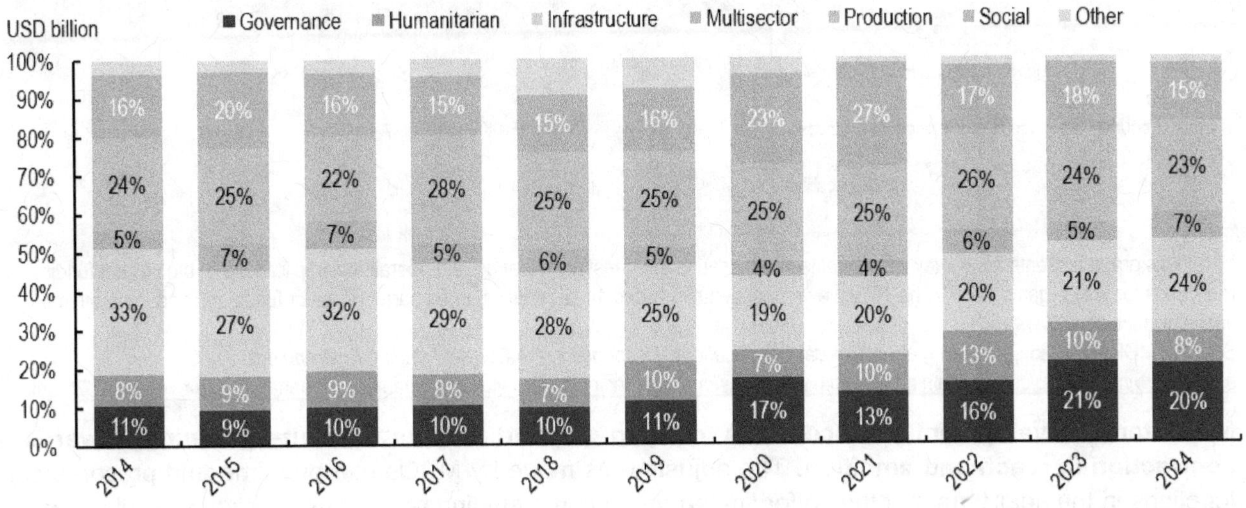

Note: Calculations are based on commitments, in 2023 constant prices. Calculations include ODA loans, ODA grants, OOF (excluding export credits), equity investment, and private sector instruments (PSI).
Source: Authors' calculations based on OECD (2026[3]), *Creditor Reporting System* (dataset), https://data-explorer.oecd.org/s/52.

With mounting financial pressures likely to materialise in coming years, the next section turns to the potential implications of the current aid crisis for multilateral delivery, examining how funding reductions could translate into outflow contraction, delivery failures and shifts in allocation.

4.2. The coming squeeze raises implications for multilateral outflows

4.2.1. *Impacts on the system's reach and ambition may be substantial and lasting*

Many multilateral development organisations are resorting to adjustment measures to absorb the funding shock, but there are likely to be impacts on development effectiveness. Across the system, MDOs have introduced hiring freezes and staff reductions, withdrawn budgeted job positions, reduced travel, relocated functions to lower-cost duty stations and deferred planned expenditures. These measures aim to preserve frontline delivery while containing administrative costs. However, available evidence suggests that the savings generated are generally insufficient to offset the magnitude of projected funding reductions and cannot avoid impacts on organisations' delivery capacities. Evidence from a 2025 survey of multilateral organisations indicates that most MDOs are experiencing programme delays, reduced geographic coverage, lower delivery targets, diminished engagement with partners and the closure of country offices (MOPAN, 2025[4]). In addition, MOPAN's analysis indicates that funding cuts are also placing pressure on MDOs' upstream functions that are less visible but still critical to development effectiveness, such as policy support, knowledge work, monitoring and evaluation, oversight and norm-setting.

Figure 4.8. More than 70% of survey respondents anticipate scaling back or suspending projects due to funding cuts

Operational implications of current funding reductions to MDOs

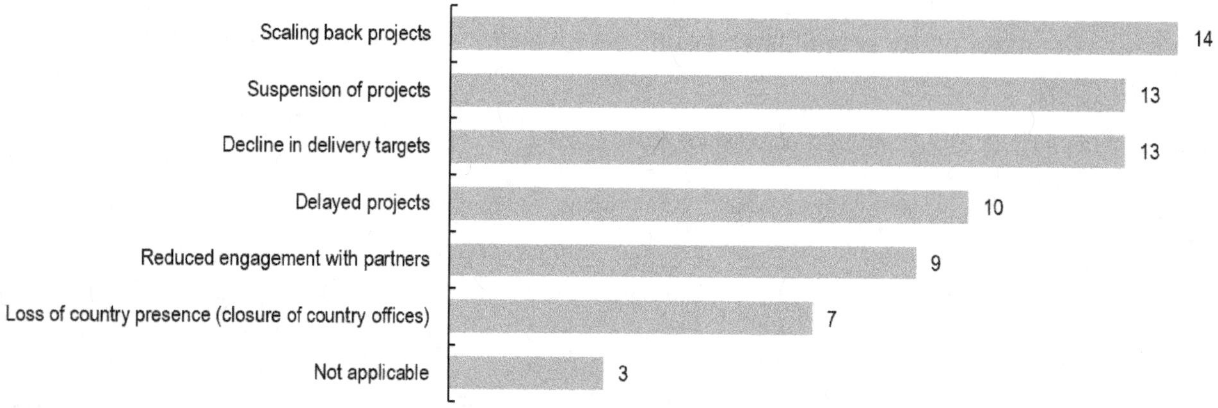

Note: This graph presents the survey respondents' responses to the question "What are the operational implications of the current funding reductions for your organisation?". The 18 survey respondents included 14 UN entities, three partnerships or funds and one international financial institution.
Source: (MOPAN, 2025[4]), *Mapping of Multilateral Organisations' Response to the Current Funding Environment*, https://www.mopan.org/content/dam/mopan/en/publications/our-work/insights/thematic-briefs/mapping/mopan-mapping-exercise-2025.pdf.

Multilateral development finance risks moving beyond temporary belt-tightening towards a contraction in reach and ambition. The adjustments made by MDOs can buy time and preserve core functions in the near term, but they offer limited protection if funding reductions persist, particularly where cuts affect predictable, multi-year funding streams. As flexibility, institutional memory and surge capacity erode, organisations may find it increasingly difficult to respond rapidly to country's needs and emerging development challenges. This shift carries risks not only for operational outputs and mandate fulfilment, but also for transparency, accountability and stakeholders' trust in the capacity of multilateral institutions.

For organisations highly dependent on voluntary grants, funding cuts are already reducing their capacity to respond to existing needs. In 2025, WFP announced that funding reductions could result in 16.7 million people losing access to emergency food assistance, including 4.8 million people in Yemen, 2.5 million in Afghanistan, and 1.6 million in Somalia (WFP, 2025[8]). Similarly, UNICEF indicated that funding cuts could force an additional 6 million children out of school (UNICEF, 2025[14]), while UNHCR has warned that 11.6 million people risk losing humanitarian assistance as a result of reduced funding (UNHCR, 2025[15]).

For replenished and leveraged mechanisms, the main risk is not immediate collapse but reverse leverage, where small funding cuts translate into larger falls in outflows in the medium term. A defining advantage of MDB concessional windows and certain funds is that each dollar of donor contribution can translate into several dollars of financing. When contributions fall, however, this multiplier can work in reverse: a one-dollar reduction in funding can translate into a larger reduction in available financing capacity (Figure 4.9). In line with the prisoner's dilemma described in Chapter 2, cutting funding for leveraged instruments like ADF, IDA and IFAD may seem attractive as it can yield budgetary savings in the short term for member states, but it comes at the expense of substantially larger costs in terms of foregone investment in the poorest and most vulnerable countries. Donors should therefore account for reverse leverage effects in budget decisions and assess the scale of foregone financing and their downstream consequences, including for debt sustainability.

Figure 4.9. Defunding multilateral leveraged mechanisms risks generating outflow losses that far exceed the budgetary savings achieved

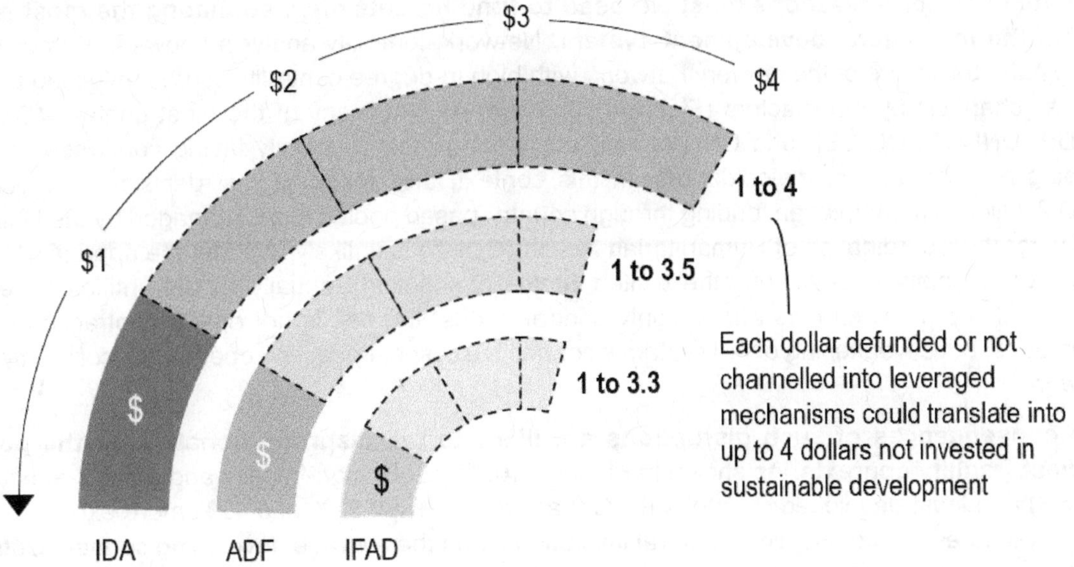

Source: IFAD (2025[16]), *2025 Report on IFAD's Development Effectiveness*, https://webapps.ifad.org/members/eb/145/docs/english/EB-2025-145-R-19.pdf?attach=1; African Development Bank (2025[17]), "African Development Fund mobilises a historic $11 billion, marking a new era of African ownership and investment-led development", https://www.afdb.org/en/news-and-events/press-releases/african-development-fund-mobilises-historic-11-billion-marking-new-era-african-ownership-and-investment-led-development-89755; World Bank Group (2023[18]), *IDA20 Mid-term Review*, https://thedocs.worldbank.org/en/doc/f1d0b477064fadf03bd4e4aa96b5b63d-0410012023/original/ida-20-MTR-factsheet-11-16-2020.pdf.

Importantly, recognising the risks of reverse leverage should not translate into a narrow focus on protecting existing mechanisms alone. It also highlights the need to use scarce capital more strategically across the system. In a constrained environment there may be scope to enhance catalytic effects beyond traditional MDB windows, provided this is done without diluting mandates or exacerbating duplication. Options could include: (i) exploring whether some vertical funds could integrate limited leveraging features where consistent with their mandates; (ii) consolidating the numerous trust funds hosted in MDBs and assessing whether part of these resources could be redeployed as capital to expand lending headroom (Lee, 2026[19]); and (iii) strengthening structured co-financing arrangements between grant-based and leveraged entities to maximise the use of scarce concessional resources.

While funding reductions constrain delivery by individual organisations, their implications extend well beyond the institutional level. The multilateral development system operates as an interconnected delivery chain in which bilateral development partners, UNDS entities, vertical funds and IFIs rely on one another to implement their mandates (Chapter 2). In such a system, cuts targeted at some key institutions may generate ripple effects across the system and to the countries they serve. The following section examines how uncoordinated funding reductions to central MDOs risk weakening not only individual organisations, but also the collective delivery capacity of the entire multilateral system.

4.2.2. Uncoordinated funding cuts to central multilateral channels risk triggering system-wide delivery failures

The multilateral development system functions as an interdependent delivery chain in which disruptions at central nodes can reverberate far beyond their own programmes. Bilateral donors rely heavily on UNDS entities to implement humanitarian and development programmes. Vertical funds depend on MDBs and UNDS entities as implementing partners for green and health financing. Normative agencies, such as WHO and ILO shape standards and frameworks that other development actors operationalise. In this architecture, funding shocks to one part of the delivery chain can disrupt multiple layers simultaneously.

Several of the organisations most exposed to funding cuts are also among the most relied upon within the multilateral development system. Network centrality analysis shows that traditional MDOs remain the backbone of the delivery network, with high in-degree centrality scores reflecting their frequent use as channels by other actors (Figure 4.10, Panel A). Yet many of the most central MDOs, such as UNDP, UNHCR, UNICEF and UN Women, are among those currently facing confirmed or anticipated funding reductions from major donors. In this context, the United States' decision to allocate around USD 2 billion in humanitarian funding through country-based pooled funds managed by the United Nations Office for the Coordination of Humanitarian Affairs (OCHA) is unlikely to offset the approximately USD 10 billion of voluntary contributions the United States channelled annually to UN entities in recent years (Lynch, 2026[20]). When cuts affect highly central nodes, the risk is not only a contraction of their own operations, but a weakening of the system's connective tissue, impacting operational continuity across the network.

The consequences of such disruptions are likely to fall disproportionately on the poorest and highest fragility contexts. As shown in Figure 4.10, Panel B, high-fragility and conflict-affected settings (FCAS) and least developed countries (LDCs) are respectively 52% and 42% more exposed to potential delivery failures from these highly central institutions than the average developing country. Cuts to central multilateral actors therefore risk amplifying financing gaps precisely where needs are greatest and substitution by other actors is least feasible.

Figure 4.10. Cuts affecting central MDOs could significantly impair the system's capacity to support the most in need

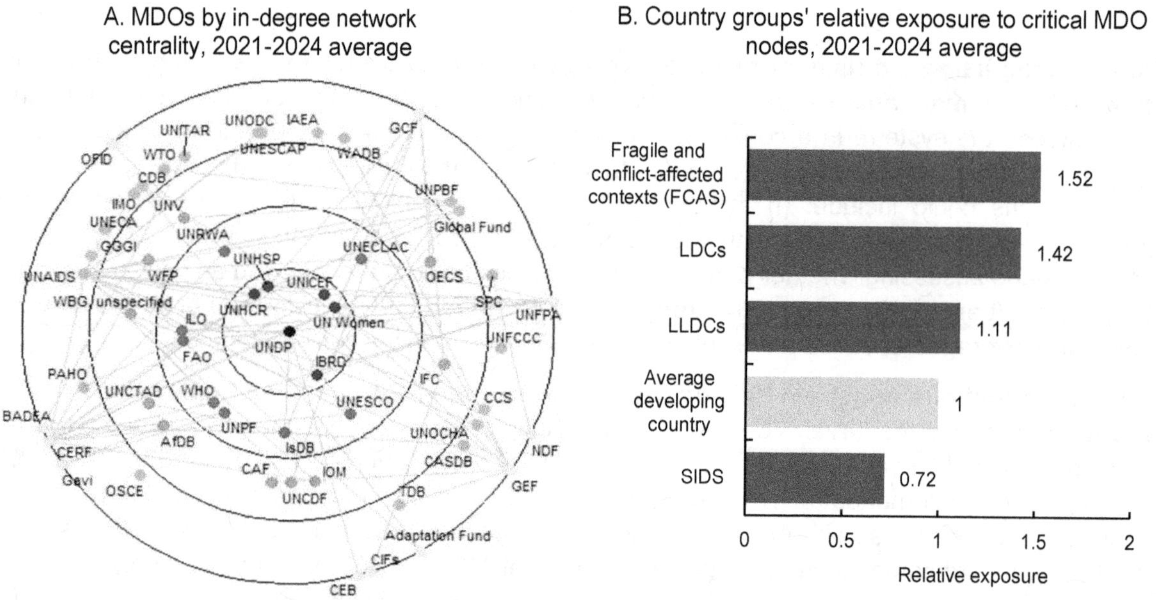

Note: In Panel A, in-degree network centrality measures how many incoming connections an organisation receives from others in the network. Applied here to the network of multilateral development organisations, it highlights which MDOs are most frequently relied upon as delivery channels within the multilateral development system. MDOs with the highest network centrality scores appear in the inner circles of the network graph and are represented in darker colours. Panel B shows the relative exposure of the most vulnerable country groups to potential delivery failures by MDOs that both exhibit a high in-degree centrality score and are affected by current funding reductions, namely: UNHCR, UNICEF, United Nations Human Settlements Programme (UNHSP), UNDP and UN Women. LDC=least-developed country; LLDC=landlocked developing country; SIDS=small island developing state.
Source: Authors' calculations based on OECD (2026[3]), *Creditor Reporting System* (dataset), https://data-explorer.oecd.org/s/52.

Uncoordinated funding cuts may generate domino effects. When individual donors reduce support to specific institutions without considering system-wide interdependencies, the resulting impacts may extend to their own earmarked contributions as well as to programmes financed by other donors. Funding decisions that focus narrowly on institutional envelopes rather than system-wide roles risk weakening the very mechanisms through which donors pursue their strategic and humanitarian objectives.

To mitigate these risks, funding decisions should account explicitly for systemic spillovers and downstream distributional impacts. In a constrained funding environment, safeguarding central delivery nodes may be essential to preserve the coherence and effectiveness of the system as a whole. For their part, MDOs can strengthen the evidence base on their system roles (e.g. pooled financing efficiencies and implementing capacity in fragile contexts) to clarify the implications of funding reductions.

Beyond the risk of delivery chain disruptions, the current funding environment may also reshape where and how multilateral resources are allocated. While this section has highlighted the systemic implications of cutting central actors, an equally important question concerns the direction of remaining resources. In a context of fiscal tightening and heightened scrutiny of value for money, MDOs may face incentives to prioritise contexts and instruments that maximise visible financial returns. This dynamic risks compounding existing shifts in the composition of multilateral development finance away from countries and sectors where development returns are highest but financial leverage is limited.

4.2.3. Concessional resources are at risk, with consequences for the most vulnerable

Multilateral organisations have demonstrated a strong capacity to support the most vulnerable countries and to engage in high priority sectors. The system does this by using concessional finance (ODA grants and loans), which is essential for its capacity to intervene in lower income countries and key sectors, especially those critical to human development. As illustrated in Figure 4.11, Panel A, in 2024 concessional financing represented 93% of total multilateral outflows received by LICs. In contrast, concessional financing accounted for only 39% of development finance received by LMICs and 27% of the total in UMICs. As illustrated in Figure 4.11, Panel B, the humanitarian and social sectors rely heavily on concessional financing, which accounts for 84% of financing in the humanitarian sector and 60% in the social sector.

Figure 4.11. Low-income countries and humanitarian and social sectors are particularly exposed to cuts in multilateral concessional finance

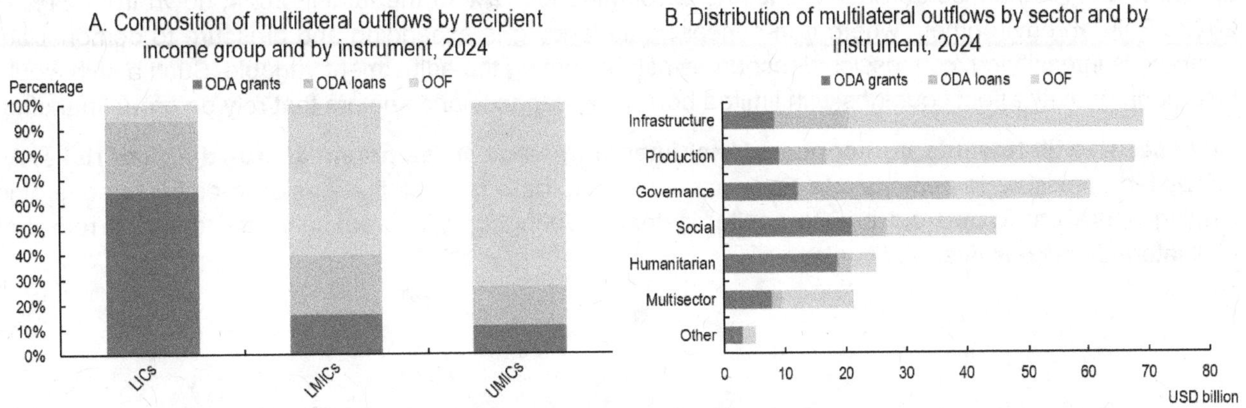

Note: Calculations are based on commitments, in 2023 constant prices. Charts illustrate volumes of ODA loans, ODA grants, and OOF (excluding export credits) but do not display equity investment and private sector instruments (PSIs), which represent marginal shares of total volumes. These components are nevertheless included in the calculations presented in the text. LIC=low-income country; LMIC=lower-middle income country; UMIC=upper-middle income country.
Source: Authors' calculations based on OECD (2026[3]), *Creditor Reporting System* (dataset), https://data-explorer.oecd.org/s/52.

Declining bilateral ODA, particularly to the poorest and most vulnerable countries, raises fundamental questions about the evolving role of multilateral development finance. Recent OECD projections show that least developed countries (LDCs) could face a 13% to 25% decline in net bilateral ODA in 2025 compared to 2023 levels, while sub-Saharan African could see reductions of 16-28% (OECD, 2025[9]). Multilateral development organisations play a critical role in these contexts: in 2023, nearly half of ODA to LDCs was channelled through multilateral development organisations. As bilateral aid contracts, the relative importance of multilateral channels in sustaining support to these countries could further increase.

Similarly, multilateral organisations are likely to assume a central role in preserving support for essential sectors that are particularly exposed to funding pressures. Humanitarian, social and governance sectors rely predominantly on grants and concessional finance, which generate limited or no financial returns and therefore rely more on public aid budgets, making them more exposed to reductions in periods of fiscal constraint. Available projections suggest that these sectors will be among the most severely affected by aid cuts. Bilateral ODA for health is projected to decline by 19-33 % in 2025 compared with 2023 levels, falling below pre-COVID-19 levels (OECD, 2025[9]). Over the same period, humanitarian assistance (including both bilateral and multilateral aid) is projected to fall by 21-36%, while ODA for education is expected to decline by 18-22%, with primary education being particularly affected (OECD, 2025[9]).

This evolving landscape calls for a clearer articulation of complementarity between bilateral and multilateral development finance. Bilateral ODA is increasingly influenced by domestic, geopolitical and strategic considerations, including security priorities, such as support to Ukraine, migration-related spending, and in-donor refugee costs. As a result, bilateral allocations may become shorter-term or politically prioritised. In this context, multilateral development finance has the potential to serve as a stabilising anchor, preserving engagement in underfunded regions, maintaining support to global public goods and ensuring continuity in the most vulnerable contexts where bilateral providers scale back. However, this stabilising role cannot be taken for granted. If multilateral concessional finance retrenches in parallel to bilateral ODA, the result would be a compounding effect on vulnerable countries.

The risk is not only a reduction in total aid volumes, but a hollowing out of concessional support where it matters the most. Concessional finance (ODA grants and concessional loans) has declined as a share of total multilateral development finance over the past decade, falling from 52% in 2014 to 46% in 2024 (Figure 4.12). This decline has been driven primarily by a reduction in the share of ODA grants, which represented around one third of total multilateral development finance in 2021-22 but fell to 26-27% in 2023-24. ODA loans also declined modestly, accounting for 19% of the total in 2024, down from 21% in 2022-23. In an environment where non-concessional lending is expanding and pressure to demonstrate leverage is intensifying, concessional resources risk becoming the adjustment variable. Such a shift would disproportionately affect countries with limited borrowing capacity and sectors that rely on grant financing.

An excessive tilt towards non-concessional financing also carries potential crowding out risks. As MDOs face pressure to demonstrate scale and leverage, there is a risk that easier-to-disburse sovereign lending operations crowd out private capital instead of bringing it in, weakening the catalytic role that multilateral finance is intended to play.

Figure 4.12. More than half of multilateral development finance delivered is now non-concessional

Evolution of multilateral development finance by instrument, 2014-2024

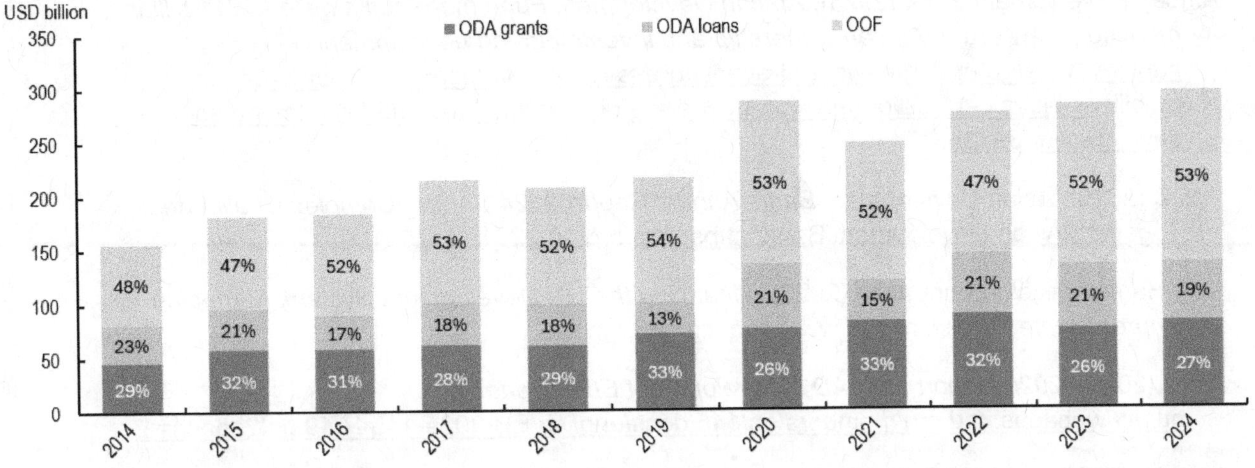

Note: ODA: official development assistance; OOF: other official flows (excluding export credits). Calculations are based on commitments, in 2023 constant prices. Calculations include ODA loans, ODA grants, OOF (excluding export credits), equity investment and private sector instruments (PSI). Equity investment and PSI are not shown in the chart since they represent marginal shares but were considered a part of total multilateral development aid when calculating the shares of ODA grants, ODA loans and OOF in total aid.
Source: Authors' calculations based on OECD (2026[3]), *Creditor Reporting System* (dataset), https://data-explorer.oecd.org/s/52.

Making best use of scarce multilateral concessional resources therefore becomes a strategic imperative. Concessional finance should be treated as a strategic input that enables engagement where risks are high and social returns exceed financial returns. First, by safeguarding concessional envelopes for LICs, LDCs and fragile and conflict-affected settings, including through minimum allocation floors or income-weighted safeguards in allocation frameworks. Second, by protecting financing for areas that underpin long-term development but generate limited financial leverage, such as humanitarian action, basic services, human capital and institution-building. Without such discipline, the system risks drifting towards easier-to-finance contexts and sectors, reinforcing the very inequalities that multilateral development finance is designed to mitigate. Doing so requires managing a fundamental tension between deploying scarce public resources where they can mobilise the greatest volume of additional capital and directing them to contexts where no other sources of finance are available.

Preserving concessional capacity is also essential for sustaining the system's legitimacy and development additionality. The comparative advantage of MDOs lies not only in scale and leverage, but in their ability to operate where bilateral providers withdraw and where private capital does not flow. If concessional finance shrinks, multilateral institutions may appear increasingly indistinguishable from other official providers, weakening their claim to development additionality.

In this context, multilateral development stakeholders face a pivotal choice. They can let multilateral development finance retrench alongside bilateral ODA, amplifying financing gaps in the poorest and most fragile countries, or they can use it as a counterweight, preserving concessional support where bilateral engagement declines. The outcome will depend on whether donors treat multilateral contributions as residual budget items or as instruments of system stewardship, and on whether MDOs align allocation decisions with explicit distributional and vulnerability objectives.

References

African Development Bank (2025), *African Development Fund mobilises a historic $11 billion, marking a new era of African ownership and investment-led development*, https://www.afdb.org/en/news-and-events/press-releases/african-development-fund-mobilises-historic-11-billion-marking-new-era-african-ownership-and-investment-led-development-89755. [17]

AsDB (2025), *Asian Development Bank: Annual Report 2024 Solving Complex Challenges Together*, Asian Development Bank, https://doi.org/10.22617/fls250100. [5]

Dag Hammarskjöld Foundation (2025), *Financing the UN Development System: Managing Unprecedented times*, https://www.financingun.report/. [6]

IFAD (2025), *2025 Report on IFAD's Development Effectiveness*, https://webapps.ifad.org/members/eb/145/docs/english/EB-2025-145-R-19.pdf?attach=1. [16]

Lee, N. (2026), ""CAF 2.0: The next callenges for MDB capital adequacy", https://www.cgdev.org/publication/caf-20-next-challenges-mdb-capital-adequacy#_edn2. [19]

Lynch, C. (2026), *Exclusive: Inside US-UN plan to remake funding for humanitarian crises*, https://www.devex.com/news/exclusive-inside-us-un-plan-to-remake-funding-for-humanitarian-crises-111682. [20]

MOPAN (2025), *Mapping of Multilateral Organisations' Response to the Current Funding Environment*, Multilateral Organisation Performance Assessment Network, Paris, https://www.mopan.org/en/our-work/performance-insights/multilateral-effectiveness-in-a-shifting-landscape/mapping-thematic-brief.html. [4]

MOPAN (2024), *Performance at a Glance: World Food Programme (WFP)*, Multilateral Organisation Performance Assessment Network, Paris, https://www.mopan.org/en/our-work/performance-evidence/wfp.html. [10]

OECD (2026), *Creditor Reporting System (dataset)*, https://data-explorer.oecd.org/s/52 (accessed on 15 January 2026). [3]

OECD (2025), "Cuts in official development assistance: OECD projections for 2025 and the near term", *OECD Policy Briefs*, No. 26, OECD Publishing, Paris, https://doi.org/10.1787/8c530629-en. [9]

OECD (2024), *Multilateral Development Finance 2024*, OECD Publishing, Paris, https://doi.org/10.1787/8f1e2b9b-en. [2]

OECD (2022), *Multilateral Development Finance 2022*, OECD Publishing, Paris, https://doi.org/10.1787/9fea4cf2-en. [1]

OECD (2020), *Multilateral Development Finance 2020*, OECD Publishing, Paris, https://doi.org/10.1787/e61fdf00-en. [11]

UNHCR (2025), "UNHCR: As funding cuts bite, some 11m people are losing aid", *Briefing Notes*, https://www.unhcr.org/news/briefing-notes/unhcr-funding-cuts-bite-some-11m-people-are-losing-aid. [15]

UNICEF (2025), "Funding cuts could push 6 million more children out of school, warns UNICEF", *UN News*, https://news.un.org/en/story/2025/09/1165764#:~:text=village%20in%20Mali.-,Funding%20cuts%20could%20push%206%20million,out%20of%20school%2C%20warns%20UNICEF&text=Global%20education%20funding%20is%20facing,(UNICEF)%20warned%20on%20Wednesday. [14]

WFP (2025), *Food Security Impact of Reduction in WFP Funding*, https://docs.wfp.org/api/documents/WFP-0000166581/download/. [8]

World Bank (2026), *World Bank Country and Lending Groups (dataset)*, https://datahelpdesk.worldbank.org/knowledgebase/articles/906519-world-bank-country-and-lending-groups. [12]

World Bank (2024), *World Bank Country Classifications by Income Level for 2024-2025 (dataset)*, https://blogs.worldbank.org/en/opendata/world-bank-country-classifications-by-income-level-for-2024-2025. [13]

World Bank Group (2023), *IDA20 Mid-term Review*, World Bank Group, Washington DC, https://thedocs.worldbank.org/en/doc/f1d0b477064fadf03bd4e4aa96b5b63d-0410012023/original/ida-20-MTR-factsheet-11-16-2020.pdf. [18]

World Bank, FAO and WFP (2025), *Strengthening Strategic Grain Reserves to Enhance Food Security*, World Bank, Washington DC, https://openknowledge.worldbank.org/server/api/core/bitstreams/9b5e0861-e981-4f9e-820a-84030ed1d981/content. [7]

www.ingramcontent.com/pod-product-compliance
Lightning Source LLC
LaVergne TN
LVHW060453061126
851857LV00016B/1818